GIGI & BUCKWHEAT

YAP

BACK-TO-SCHOOL

Dogs' Life:
The Magazine for Today's Dog
by Heidi A. Ott

First Edition

Copyright ©2003 by Heidi A. Ott.

River bank press

Published by:
Riverbank Press
311 Jethro Lane
Yorktown, Virginia 23692
www.riverbankpress.com

Printed in Hong Kong
by Magnum (Offset)
Printing Co. Ltd.

Book design by Saxon Design Inc.,
Traverse City, Michigan

Library of Congress
Control Number: 2003093912

Ott, Heidi A.
Dogs' Life: The Magazine for Today's Dog/
Heidi A. Ott
ISBN 0-9728991-0-3
1. Dogs
2. Humor

DOGS' LIFE

Alpha Editor: BOO OTT

Big Dog Publisher: HURLEY GRRRRLY BROWN

Top Dog Assistant: PAWS CARTWRIGHT

Contributors
F. SCOTTY FITZGERALD, TOM WOLFHOUND, EDWARD LABBEY, HEBE WHITE, GEORGE BERNARD PAW, ELISABETH BASSET BROWNING, DOGDEN NASH

Leader of the Pack
NEAPOLITAN BONEPART

Obedience Director
GEN. NORDOG SCHWARSCHNAUZER

Trackers
THE GERMAN SHORTHAIRED POINTER SISTERS

Story Retrievers
LARRY BIRD-DOG, GOLDIE HANN RETRIEVER, HELEN HUNTER

Left Field Correspondent
BABE RUFF

Staff Shepherd
MARY SHELTIE

Arty Dogs
PABLO PUGCASSO, SALVADOR DOGI, MONA LHASA

Research Pack
AL CHOKER, BONE PHILIPS, ALDUS HUSKY, JANE PAWLEY, SNOOPY

Pedigree Consultant
CAVALIER PRINCE CHARLES SPANIEL

Fashion Consultants
RAQUEL WELSH CORGI, BILL BLASSETHOUND, COCO KHANEL, FLEAMAN MARCOS, IZDOG

Fur Stylists
COLLIE PARTON, BEN FUR

Legal Affairs Wolves
CASPER WEIMARANER, HARRY S. TRUEDOG

Propaganda Pack
FIDO CASTRO, WOODROVER WILSON, TRENT SPOT

Dog Fight Coordinators
TYKE TYSON, MALAMUTE ALI, PHYLLIS KILLER

Escape Consultant
HOUNDINI

Walkies Advisor
FRED ASTAIRDALE

Barkers
DINGO STAR, MARIA COLLARS, DORIS STRAY, ARFIE SHAW, GORDON LIGHTFOOT SETTER

Financial Advisors
THE MOTLEY DROOL

Howling Consultants
THE BARKS BROTHERS, STRAY LENO, BILL FURRY, SNOOPY GOLDBERG, BARK TWAIN

Executive Shredders: CHEWY LEWIS AND THE CHEWZ, THE PLAYFUL SHRED

Food Tasters
BETTY COCKER, WOLFGANG PUG, JAMES BRIARD, THE RUNAWAY GOURMET, DR. DROOLITTLE, FAITHFUL BREAD

Bone Tester: SUNNY BON-O

Under Dog: ODIE

Associate Under Dog: ROMIN' PAWLANSKI

Lap Dogs
LICKEY ROONY, MICHAEL J. FOXHOUND, TERRIER GARR, BEN AFLATACK, BRAD PITBULL

Spiritual Advisors
RIN TIN TIN, BENJI, OLD YELLER, BINGO, CHIPS, PRINCE, SHEP and LASSIE

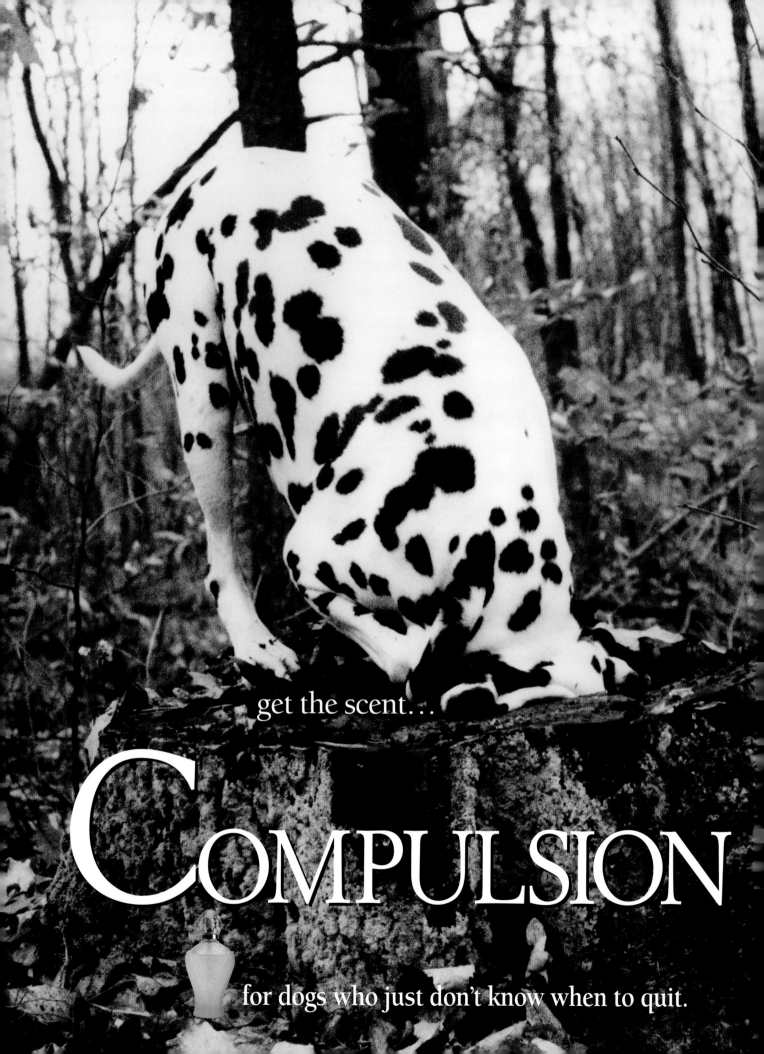

contents

features

field notes

table scraps

playtime

pointers

about our
Contributors

Rover Washington,

a descendent of President George Washington's famous hounds, shares his Georgetown brownstone with his human (a retired White House kennel worker). The aristocratic Dachshund is considered one of the foremost authorities on Presidential canines, and actually sniffed Buddy Clinton shortly before his untimely demise in 2002. "I wrote ALL THE PRESIDENTS' DOGS (page 57),"explains Rover, "in the hopes that my fellow canines might gain an appreciation for the many contributions Presidential pooches have made to our country, and perhaps aspire to become a political animal themselves one day."

Smellany Post

is a regular contributor to DOGS' LIFE magazine. After visiting numerous dog parks during a summer road trip with her humans, Ms. Post felt compelled to write DOG PARK ETIQUETTE (page 32). "I just love a good dog park," said the above Standard Poodle, "and most of the time everyone runs smoothly. Occasionally, however, I am shocked by the beastly manners of some of my canine cohorts. Therefore, I took it upon myself to dictate proper dog park etiquette so that the more well-heeled among us can enjoy our park experiences without being unnecessarily offended."

Mooch Fillmore

teaches beginning through advanced begging at Canine Academy, and is the best-selling author of "Even Beggars Can Be Choosers" (published by *Appeal To The Chair Press*). In his article, THE 7 HABITS OF HIGHLY EFFECTIVE BEGGARS (page 24), this big yellow Lab offers up seven safe, easy and effective ways to acquire better tastes. According to Mooch, "Most Dogs never learn how to beg effectively; they develop bad begging habits as pups, and never move beyond the tid-bit stage. My article will help any Dog—who truly desires it— to become a better beggar."

SheBear de la Laisse

is a free-lance Schipperke and self-described thrill-seeker. She recently spent nearly 24 hours sans leash, exploring nearly every facet of her hometown of Seattle, Washington. "It wasn't like I planned it," said SheBear. "The gate latch was broken and temptation just got the better of me." During her day off-leash, SheBear explored over 15 miles of her home town, from the watery depths of the Hiram M. Chittenden Locks, to the dizzying heights of the Space Needle. "After that, I was grounded," SheBear admitted, "but it gave me plenty of time to write LEASH-LESS IN SEATTLE (page 47)." The action-packed adventure story is her first foray into the memoir genre.

Dr. Baily MacGrowell,

a Bearded collie from Scotland, Illinois, has been foiling members of the feline persuasion ever since puppy-hood, when his domestic bliss was catastrophically disrupted by the unexpected arrival of an uncouth kitten from the local SPCA. His article, GIVING PUSS THE BOOT (page 69), is the culmination of 35 dog years of in-depth scientific experiments in the field of feline behavior modification. "Believe it or not," says McGrowell, "cats now outrank us dogs as the #1 American pet. I feel it is up to the canine community to reverse this trend, and I hope my article contributes to this end."

a letter from the Alpha Editor

"It's a dog's life." So said a deep-thinker named Erasmus (I know, Erasmus would be a good name for a Terrier, huh?). But this was an old Dutchman who coined the phrase around 1542 (aaarrf, that's over 3,000 dog-years ago!). Although I can't tell you if Mr. E. ever owned a dog himself, he apparently thought that the dogs of his day lived under pretty miserable conditions. When you think about it—no can-openers, no dog parks, no Frisbees, no flea control—he was probably right.

Times have changed though, thank Dog! These days—because of the adoring humans who pamper their four-legged friends with toys and treats, fun and games, warm beds and even massages—many of us dogs are living on cloud K-9.

But, unfortunately, not all of us. Here's a bit of information that will put your tail between your legs: The Humane Society of the United States (your Political Action Committee!) estimates that the number of dogs and cats that go into animal shelters every year (that's a human year, of course) is around six to eight million (you will never see that many Milk-Bones even if you live to be 100). But, wait, it gets worse! About half of all those poor, hapless curs and kitties end up receiving capital punishment! What was their crime, you ask? Well, maybe they were born to some stray bitch who didn't have any birth control, and so they ended up a stray as well. Maybe they were purchased from a pet store by some human who didn't know what he was getting into, and once the puppy love wore off that human decided to dump Rover at the pound. Or, maybe they ran away from an unhappy (as in cruel and unusual) home. Obviously, none of these are actual crimes. Nonetheless, they are big reasons why so many dogs and cats end up in animal shelters, living a less than perfect life.

Why am I going on and on about this dismal topic, you ask? Because as Alpha Editor of DOGS' LIFE magazine I feel it is my responsibility not only to entertain my readers, but to help them become more responsible pets as well. My dream is to live in a world where every dog has his day. Where all of my canine brethren have happy, loving homes, and enjoy three (or more) square meals a day, regular walkies with unbridled access to p-mail, sofa privileges, daily tummy rubs, and an open charge account at Petsmart. For that to happen, though, we must make those animal shelters a thing of the past.

You can do your part. To start with, we need to reproduce responsibly to reduce our ranks, so, if you haven't already, insist that you get spayed or neutered (it's really not so bad). Next, take your human through at least basic obedience; that way he or she will learn to understand you and how your doggy brain works, and the two of you will form a better and a more long-lasting bond. If you hear about a pet in trouble, report it to the nearest ASPCA. And last but not least, if your family decides to get another furry friend, demand (howl, yap, but put your paw down) that they visit the local animal shelter and take home one (or more) of the many loveable, deserving, eager pets (about a quarter of which are pure bred!) that are available every day. If we all do these simple things, the problem of pet over-population and suffering will disappear. Then maybe our humans will figure out how to solve their own species over-population and suffering problems!

Okay, I'll get down off my soap box now (after chewing on it the other day it's not as stable as it used to be), and let you get on with reading the rest of the magazine. It's a cool issue, if I do say so myself! My good friend, Mooch Fillmore explains the 7 HABITS OF HIGHLY EFFECTIVE BEGGARS; Dr. Baily MacGrowell shows you how to give PUSS THE BOOT; Smellany Post dictates DOG PARK ETIQUETTE; Rover Washington reveals some interesting tid-bits about ALL THE PRESIDENTS' DOGS; and SheBear de la Laisse takes you for the romp of your life in her short story, "LEASH-LESS IN SEATTLE."

Keep on waggin'!

Boo Ott

BOO'S SOAP
Leaves dogs so Loveable!

"I don't believe in the concept of hell, but if I did I would think of it as filled with people who were cruel to animals."
—Gary Larson

Club Shed
let it all fall out!

- **To-drool-for dishes** prepared by our noted canine chefs
- **Over-stuffed sofa beds** and **cable TV** in every den
- Refreshing **fresh and saltwater swimming**
- **Real sheep herding** on the open range
- Unlimited **tummy rubs** and **no-leash walkies**
- Huge selection of **chewing toys**
- Exciting **car-chasing pits**

Club Shed

readers' rebarks:
dear DOGS' LIFE

CREATIVE CROTCH SNIFFING

Thanks to Wolfie Noseback's fascinating article on crotch sniffing, I feel like a new dog! I used to worry constantly about my fixation on crotches until I read that crotch sniffing occupies up to 92% of some Dogs' waking hours. Thank you, Wolfie! —Your loyal fan, Nosy Parker

Wolfie hit it bang on again. He is absolutely the most observant and thorough reporter on your staff. First, I had no idea that crotch sniffing had such a long and complex history. And I never would have thought that Rin Tin Tin and other great film Canines were such avid sniffers. His article gave me a whole new appreciation of the art.—Woody Loon

I cannot tell you how inspired I was after reading "Creative Crotch Sniffing!" I had been going about it all wrong, but I'm on the right track now.
—Lilith Chips

As a mature Basset Hound, I found the article by Wolfie Noseback, "Creative Crotch Sniffing," intelligently written, decidedly useful and just downright fun to read.
—Ozwald Olephant

HEAD OVER HEELS

Your article, "Head Over Heels," gave me paws to think about the hidden dangers of the Frisbee®. I did not know that Frisbees are as addictive as tennis balls and that a Dog (except a Labrador retriever), once hooked, will willingly pass up food in order to keep playing. Important information for all of us. As usual, DOGS' LIFE is cutting edge.
—Fifi O'Hair

About your article, "Head Over Heels," is it really true that some Dogs have played Frisbee for three days straight? If so, where did they find the human who could throw for so long, and can you please send me that human's address?
—MadDog Chasingham

HUMAN PACK DYNAMICS

Thank you for the brilliant, educational and timely article, "Human Pack Dynamics," by Franz Furbull. Dr. Furbull described my own human pack perfectly. Now I better understand their confusing body language. Obviously, humans are not nearly as advanced as they think they are.
—Zelda Pogwistle

I don't know where that Dr. Furbull gets his information, but I wanna tell you (or him) that he's full of artificial ingredients. The humans I hang out with don't act anything like what he says they should.
—King Kong, K9 Unit, Idlewild Sherriff's Dept.

SNOW DOGS

I am a Siberian Husky. I live in Key West, Florida. I have never seen snow (except on TV). After reading the chilling article Snow Dogs, I hope I never do. Keep up the good work.
—Sundancer

SCRATCH 'N SNIFF

I just had to write in and tell you how much I loved last month's "Meatloaf Scratch 'n Sniff!" You should see that page—rather, what is left of it. I scratched and sniffed until I was delirious, demented, and debilitated! My human had to put me in my crate for the rest of the day, but it was worth it. DOGS' LIFE magazine needs more great Scratch 'n Sniffs!—Rosie Banana

Nibbles & Bits for News Hounds
LIFE BITES

Dem Bones

It seems that long-time stray, Dusty Muttley Brown, has a new home! While scrounging around in the Long Lost Hills of Texas last month, he joined a bone-fide archaeological dig, and ended up with a human and a home of his very own. DOGS' LIFE Adventure Reporter, Scout Pawstrong, interviewed Muttley about his good fortune.

SCOUT: "Hey there, Muttley, I hear you've got yourself a brand new home and a cool new human. Righteous! So tell our readers what happened to you out in the Long Lost Hills."

MUTTLEY: "Well, Scout, it was already a killer hot mornin', and I was just sniffin' around for a little breakfast roadkill—you know, somethin' to take the edge off a belly-gnawin' hunger—when I come across a pack of humans diggin' in the sand with itty-bitty shovels and teeny-tiny whisk brooms. I figured at that rate it would take them a hundred dog-years to un-earth whatever was down there. And I, for one, was hopin' it might be a big ol' meaty rack-o-bovine ribs or somethin'. Sooo, figurin' they could use some expert help, I set to digging too. Only they got all worried-smellin' and shooed me out of their burrow, so I sniffed around and started diggin' a hole of my own. Well, shucks, the next thing I know, I'm up to my tail in sand, pullin' at one heck of a giant bone!"

SCOUT: "Cool! How big was it, Muttley?"

MUTTLEY: "Heck! (I mean Woof!) It was as big as a Labrador's appetite! Let me tell ya, I would not want to sniff the wrong end of the dog that buried that thing, know what I mean? No way could I pull it out by myself. So I start barkin', 'Hey-hey-hey, I need some help over here guys—like, any time today, okay?' Believe it or not, they just ignored me! Had their heads stuck tight in their little holes, scrapin' dirt and blowin' dust."

SCOUT: "Humans—what did they think you were barkin' for, fun?"

MUTTLEY: "Man! (I mean Dog!) I don't know. But after sittin' there howlin' over the bone for, like an hour, one of them finally comes over—I think to tell me to hush. You shoulda seen the look on that feller's face when he saw what I had in MY hole. I mean we're talkin' major 'Yip-Yip-Yip!' Then the other fellas come runnin' over to see."

SCOUT: "Far out! Then what?"

MUTTLEY: "Well, I'm pretty excited myself, so I jump back in the hole to grab the bone, see? But the guys start jumpin' up and down and shoutin' at me and gettin' real worried-smellin'. One of them pulls me out by the scruff of my neck and says to me: 'Sit! Stay!' You know, the usual yackity yack-yack."

SCOUT: "Rude dude! That was your hole, your bone."

MUTTLEY: "Yeah, I know, but they gave me a chicken salad sandwich and a bowl of water and a shady place to nap—all for just stayin' out of their way. And, bein' hungry and feelin' pretty hang-dog from all that diggin' and barkin', I figured it was a fair shake."

SCOUT: "But what about the bone, Muttley?"

MUTTLEY: "Oh they eventually got it out, and a whole lot of other bones too. Took 'em days though, workin' with those spoons and brushes. And those bones were way past their prime—no meat, no gristle, hardly any smell. I mean, this stuff had been down there waaay too long, if you know what I mean. Still, the guys were wild about it, playin' and arrangin' the bones like they were a big ol' jig-saw puzzle. They called it T. Rex, or somethin', but it sure didn't resemble no dog I'd ever seen. Tell you the truth, I sort of lost interest in it, and dug a bunch of other holes."

SCOUT: "Whoa, a bunch of humans panting over a lot of meat-less bones in the desert—sounds like a pretty bizarre sight to me!"

MUTTLEY: "It was, Scout! If you ask me, these guys had their collars adjusted a notch too tight. But they seemed to really like me; kept callin' me their 'mascot,' whatever that is. The old gray guy called Doc was especially friendly; he always made sure I was fed, and he even let me sleep next to him in his tent."

SCOUT: "Sweet! Is Doc the one who took you home? I mean, is he your new human?"

MUTTLEY: "Yep, Doc's my man! Bought me a new flea collar, and a big box of Milk-Bones. And I got my own bed in the house when we're at home, and I get to sit in the front seat of his Jeep when we go places.

SCOUT: "Sounds great Muttley! I'm sure our readers are curious though: won't you miss the freedom of the open range?"

MUTTLEY: "No way! My driftin' and dumpsterin' days are over. Livin' with Doc is bitchin'. We're always drivin' off to interestin'-smellin' new places where we dig holes all day long, sleep in a warm tent at night, and eat good chow. He scratches my ears and I lick his face. I only wish Doc would get my name right, though—he keeps callin' me Dino-Mutt."

SCOUT: "You know, Muttley, that's not such a bad name, it kind of suits you. Anyway, looks like you found yourself a happy home at last. Enjoy it, fella!"

LIFE BITES

Plastic Geese Herding Record Broken

In an unexpected upset, novice herder, Will Winkler, edged out reigning champ, Tigre Woodside, at the National Plastic Geese Herding (PGH) Championship last week. "Nobody thought Winkler could pull it off," said PGH organizer, Casper Bouvier, "but his record-breaking barking barrage made him the clear winner, paws down." Asked about his victory, a panting Will said he owed it all to proper diet, training, and a box of throat lozenges he found in the trash.

Deli Raided

The infamous gang TNT (Terribly Naughty Terriers) was tracked down and picked up by City pound officials in connection with the recent daring raid on Oscar's South Side Delicatessen. Allegedly, the gang sneaked in the back door of the deli as Oscar was closing up. Once inside they devoured the contents of the sliced meat and cheese cases before making off with a medium-rare roast beef, a honey baked ham, two BBQ chickens, and a boneless turkey roll. Officials followed a trail of egg salad to the gang's hideout behind the deli's dumpster, where they discovered the pack chewing on Alka-Seltzer tablets and whimpering with indigestion. The TNT gang is comprised of Rags "Bad Boy" White, a West Highland white terrier from the West side; Ghengas Wrong, a Jack Russell terrier from Shanghai; Francis "The Cur" O'Hair, a Norfolk terrier from Dublin; and Axel B. Roseinblat, a Bull terrier from Istanbul. Bail for each dog was set at 2,500 Milk-Bones.

"A Little Lower, Please"

The ancient art of Wolfing was practiced routinely by our wolf ancestors to realign the spine after a severe bear thrashing, to stimulate lower-brain functions impaired by excessive mating, or just to relax after a busy day of bison hunting. Now, Wolfing therapy is making a comeback at the Paws-On Therapy Institute (POTI) in San Iliac, California. At Paws-On you can enjoy the rejuvenating benefits of Wolfing in an all-natural, earthy outdoor setting. Trained Wolfing therapists will customize treatments to meet your mood and breed-specific needs. Benefits include enhanced tail-wagging, a more balanced bark, and a livelier libido.

Domestication? or Evolution?

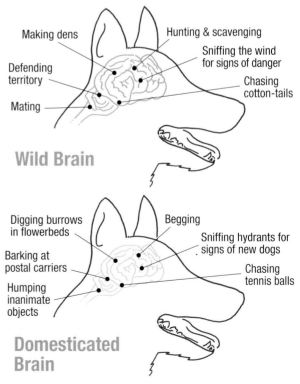

Making dens

Hunting & scavenging

Defending territory

Sniffing the wind for signs of danger

Mating

Chasing cotton-tails

Wild Brain

Digging burrows in flowerbeds

Begging

Barking at postal carriers

Sniffing hydrants for signs of new dogs

Humping inanimate objects

Chasing tennis balls

Domesticated Brain

(Diagrams courtesy of Dog Brain Research Institute)

CHUNG'S DEPILATORY CREAM

Removes unsightly hair...in a hurry

Now available in a
Convenient Spray Dispenser

Buster's Balls

To beg for a
Buster's Balls Dogalog,
contact Dogs' Life magazine
dept B

bumper stickers
we have chased...

DOG IS LOVE

My HONK is worse than my BITE

Shar-Peis hang loose

GOOD BEGGARS
CAN BE CHOOSERS

Warning! Dachshund...somewhere behind the wheel

TO ERR IS HUMAN,
TO FORGIVE CANINE

Have you licked
your Master today?

In a Shih Tzu world,
it's survival of the fluffiest

Dogs never cry over spilt milk –
they just lap it up

Always turn around 3 times
before lying down

BICHONS RULE!

MY HUMAN IS HOUSEBROKEN

If you bit off more than you can chew,
you're probably a Labrador

My Puppy is an Honor Student
at At-A-Boy Obedience School

I ♥ My Human

My human is smart as a Whippet

I'm OK, I'm a DOG

Dobermans are armed
to the teeth

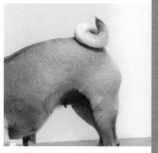

Mouth to Muzzle!

I'll be the first to admit it: I'm a lousy swimmer. The only time I ever intentionally tried to swim (it was a stupid puppy stunt) I sank straight to the bottom. Honest! Had to be dip-netted out of the kiddie pool. We Chows have thick, wooly coats that weigh a ton when soaking wet, and dainty cat-like paws not well suited for the dog-paddle, and rather poor eye-sight—the result of deep-set eyes surrounded by furry brows. You may well ask, "What were the idiots who designed my breed thinking?" Well it sure wasn't water rescue work or duck retrieval. It's true, I had no business at the end of the pier that hot summer day, but the heat was killing me and, in my search for a cool breeze, I ended up out there. I must have passed out from heat frustration (or whatever they call it) and fell off the pier, because I don't remember a single thing between standing on the edge looking down into the water, and lying on the lawn looking up into the flared nostrils of my Aunt Edith. Edith had my whole muzzle in her mouth, breathing air into my nose—a delicious liverwurst smell. My mistress, Edna, and all the kids were shouting, "Ciao! Ciao! Wake up Ciao!" as Edith continued CPR (Canine Pant Recovery) on me. Wide awake, I struggled free and gave myself a good shake, spraying water all over everybody. The humans were so relieved I was alive they jumped and cheered and clapped old Edith on the back. The kids asked where she learned to give mouth-to-mouth to a dog, and Aunt Edith replied, "Oh, I just sort of made it up as I went along, dearie." After that Edna gave me my very own doggy life vest to wear near water, but I plan to stay clear of the pier from now on.

tails
of
woe

Weaned by a Cat!

When Mother, a vain, diminutive Brussels griffon, fell in love with Father, a Griff of sizeable stature, she gave little thought to the potential complications that might result from a pregnancy by him. Endowed as I was with Father's "big" genes, when the time came to make my grand entrance into the world I found it quite impossible to squeeze down Mother's petite birth canal. As a result, Mother was given general anesthesia, and the vet delivered me via caesarian section. She was still asleep as I bumbled about from her head to her tail looking for a hot toddy (or at least a warm teat). I suppose a case could be made that because Mother slept through my entire birth she could not be expected to have strong maternal instincts toward me, but she didn't even recognize me! Maybe she just wasn't cut out for motherhood. Well, there I lay, slimy, blind, hungry, and utterly rejected. Had the kindly vet not managed to smuggle me onto the milkline of a motherly cat who had just given birth to a litter of kittens in the next room, I probably wouldn't have made it to day two. Mama Cat did not object to one more mouth to feed—even if I was a strange bedfellow—and I eagerly suckled along side my new feline siblings. For several weeks life was good. I was warm and clean, and I put on considerable weight. Eventually, however, when my eyes were wide open and I was able to waddle about on my own, I was taken away from Mama Cat and the kittens, and reunited with Mother. Mother still does not recognize me, but that's her problem, and to this day I hold a very special place in my heart for kitties.

continued on page 16

tails

Down the Duct!

For a Chihuahua, living through a total home renovation project is fraught with perils. Like the day I went to inspect some recent modifications by the Heating & Cooling Man. He had cut holes in the floor of every single room, and installed shiny duct work down them all. I distinctly heard sinister sounds floating up from these ducts. I was growling and yapping staccato-like over the hole next to the front door, when my mistress rushed in to answer the doorbell. It was the vacuum cleaner salesman, and when I turned to growl at him I lost my footing on the hard-wood floor and slipped right down the duct. I felt like Alice in Wonderland, plummeting down the rabbit hole, the light shrinking rapidly away, then—WHUMP!—I hit bottom. Sure that the Duct Monster was about to grab me, I yelped and screeched at the top of my lungs and pawed frantically to get out, but couldn't get a purchase on the slick sides of the duct. I spun around in my tubular coffin, yapping in terror, for what seemed an eternity before the long arm of the Heating & Cooling Man finally reached down and plucked me out—not without a little discomfort either, I might add. My mistress grabbed me, hugged me, inspected me for damage, and cooed, "Is my little Chiquita okay?" The H&C Man put covers over all the holes soon after that, effectively entombing the fiendish Duct Monster. Sometimes though, late at night, especially when it's windy, I can still hear its sinister howls throughout the house. 🐾

DOGS' LIFE
leisure COLUMN

camp run·a·muck

Chasing a Little Tail!

Long before leashes and licenses, fences and flea collars, back when wild packs ran free, chasing tail was a popular pastime—a sport all but forgotten with the ever-increasing demands of domestication. Fortunately, with the advent of modern off-leash dog parks, the age-old game is enjoying a renaissance. If you've never chased tail before you'll find it is a wonderful way to get some healthy exercise. It's a natural stress reliever, too. And, no matter what your preference—long and fluffy, short and sleek, or even docked—chasing tail is also a fun way to embarrass your human.

Resort Getaway...

CAMP RUN-A-MUCK is the vacation run-away you've been panting for. At CAMP RUN-A-MUCK you won't know which of the exciting attractions to try first: Chase a wide variety of vermin (including chipmunks, ground squirrels and hamsters) around the professional 18-hole Critter Course. Looking for bigger game? Try tracking orphaned baby black bear (no nasty mama bear to ruin your day) through Dogwood Forest. Into herding? CAMP RUN-A-MUCK stocks herds of sheep, piglets and pre-schoolers for every experience level. Relax after a thrilling ride on the Aarff-Aarff Autobahn in CAMP RUN-A-MUCK's fully stocked chew bar where you'll find the finest selection of slippers, hand bags and sofa cushions anywhere. Call CAMP RUN-A-MUCK for reservations today! 555-BEEBAD

Bow-Wow Walkies!

Great news for all you lazy dogs out there: Now you can enjoy all the sights, sounds and smells of the great outdoors without ever lifting a leg. With the patented PICK-ME-UP HUMAN-MOUNTED CANINE CARRIER from Lazy Dog, Inc., you can ride upon master's (or mistress's) back instead of trudging along on a short leash. Imagine riding high enough to look down and laugh at all the other dogs on the block. Imagine never again being rudely jerked away from interesting-smelling objects. Nope, just sit back and enjoy the ride. And when something catches your attention just bark loudly in your human's ear—their signal to stop and let you meditate, copulate, excavate, lacerate, or urinate. Yes, all that energy you used to spend on actually walking can now be directed towards these and other more stimulating pastimes. Order your very own PICK-ME-UP HUMAN-MOUNTED CANINE CARRIER from Lazy Dog, Inc., today, and start riding high tomorrow! Training booklet included. Suggested retail price: 79.95 Milk-Bones.

bookreviews

Catch-20 Chew

🐾🐾🐾🐾

By Joseph Hellraiser (Howell House, 25 Milk-Bones)

The Cur-de-Sac Pack is back and up to their collars in trouble again. This time the raiding rovers crash a local dowsing convention where humans are practicing their skills at finding buried water with the aid of some lovely, hand-crafted divining rods. The dogs make off with all of the prize rods and get led around (literally by the nose) to a secret well containing the Fountain of Vermouth. And when the pack gets wind of the beefy delivery headed for Boris's Butcher Shop, they devise some of their most hilarious and innovative thievery tricks yet. This is Hellraiser at his wittiest; a tummy-tickler for sure.

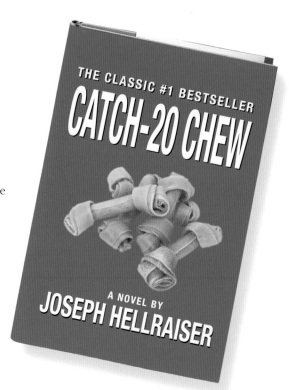

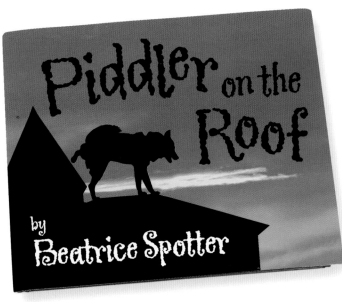

Piddler on the Roof

🐾🐾🐾🐾

By Beatrice Spotter (Puppy-Love Books, 18 Milk-Bones)

This charmingly written, beautifully illustrated book is a wonderfully way to introduce your young pups to the art and joy of marking. Piddles is a spunky, adventurous little Malamute who knows no bounds to his territory. "When it comes to marking," says Piddles to his litter mates, "the sky's the limit!" And slowly the timid siblings follow his lead—all the way up to the roof top. Appropriate for puppies 6 weeks and up. Bitches will appreciate the waterproof, chew-resistant cover.

Come Back Little Shiba Inu

By Mavis Amour (Wolf Publishing, 32 Milk-Bones)

Mavis Amour's debut novel is set in medieval Japan, where Little Shiba flees an abusive relationship with her domineering mate, Jaba, in search of true love. When Jaba wakes up and discovers Little Shiba has run away, he is devastated and begins a soul-searching trek during which he realizes that he had mistreated Little Shiba and taken her for granted. He vows to change his ways and bring her back home. Both Jaba and Little Shiba, in their separate quests for love and meaning, run into grueling obstacles: Jaba faces off with a samurai Siamese, and Little Shiba is captured by a war lord who wants to use her to hunt doves. These trials force them to dig deep inside for the strength to prevail.

A Reference for **Really Dumb Dogs**

Toilet Paper
FOR
DUMMIES

by Lou Tishue

FREE Twin-ply "Cheat Sheet" Inside!

Features include:
* Toilet Paper Origami
* Using Toilet Paper as a Fashion Accessory
* Decorating with Colored Toilet Papers
* Fun and Easy Toilet Paper Roll Derbies
* Toilet Paper Tug-O-War
* Stress-Relieving Qualities of Scented Toilet Paper

soapopera
reviews

AS THE TAIL WAGS

Sushi loses her dog tags and is picked up by Animal Control. Meanwhile, Babs becomes happily engaged to Bodie, who is scheduled to be docked. Pluto's yard is TP'd by the neighborhood brats—on his watch! Maude and Lady are left alone all day and decide to redecorate the house. After graduating with honors from Canine Academy, Harpo gets overly excited at his graduation party and is scolded for ripping up his graduation cap. Zorro gets a bath then races around the house like a mad dog and frightens the cat to death.

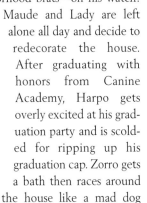

ALL MY PUPPIES

Now that she's pregnant, Daisy Mae believes she will get Newt to marry her, even though Newt has told her that he is still in love with Snow White. Henriette confronts Bulah regarding her puppy's destructive teething. Little Rock piddles on the new oriental carpet and is unceremoniously deposited outside, much to the delight of his litter mates. Dora discovers that she does not have enough teats for her entire litter and begins worrying even more about Runtly's future.

DAYS OF OUR DOGS

Maybelline hears that Axle was the Dog involved in the back alley fight and packs her bags. Beasty and Ping move in together. Pogo wanders too far away from home this time. Winnie bites Shorty for stealing her mailman squeaky toy. When Mr. Tietlebaub leaves a secret message for Lumpkin at the fire hydrant, he is seen by Cookie who vows to get even. Spot is accepted by the Seeing Eye Dog School and must face his separation anxiety. Champion Cleopatra Queen of Denial hears rumors that she is to be mated to Champion Cosmo Space Cadet and falls into a deep depression. Emma bites the mailman again.

THE GUIDING SCENT

Roosevelt is surprised when Speck shows up on his doorstep after Louella kicked him out of the dog house. Cecil urges Guido to get a heartworm test after admitting to a fling with Astrid-the-slut-bitch. Gidgit pays Rufus an unexpected visit while he's in the pound and, shocked that she is not dead, he grovels for her forgiveness, whining that he was under the influence of a full moon when he ran off and left her in the lurch. Dallas is put on the trail of a serial killer just as his allergies begin acting up.

THE YOUNG AND THE PLAYFUL

Floppy is depressed, despite Roxanne's licks and nips and bow-play postures. Meanwhile, wolves are circling around Vladimir's dog house, sent by the ruthless Samson who is eager for retribution for showing him up at the Fly Ball competition. Psycho and Rex herd a group of pre-schoolers into the back yard. Aldo plays tug of war with Muriel and loses badly. Xero finds a new tennis ball in Master's gym bag but is conflicted about taking it. Rushing out to greet Soccer Mom's van, Bently encounters the mean Maine Coon cat and is rescued in the nick of time by the Kid. Ego is dismayed to discover that his mistress has adopted a retired Greyhound and things get worse when the has-been racer is allowed to sleep on the bed.

THE VETERINARIANS

Webster goes in for routine teeth cleaning and ends up in intensive care. Zoe protests her spaying, saying she desperately wants to have Julio's puppies; however, her Mistress is unrelenting. Gertie doesn't recognize Baskerville when he arrives home wearing a white anti-scratch cone collar. In her confusion she nips his tail repeatedly, thus sending him back to the vet for reconstructive surgery. The veterinarian rules Dolly's death a suicide after she wandered off into a blinding snow storm, but the Search & Rescue Dogs find plucked chicken feathers and suspect fowl play. When the Teenager accidentally cuts one of Raoul's nails to the quick he howls bloody murder and is rushed to the emergency vet.

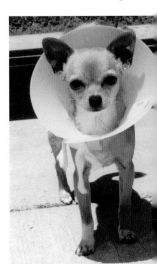

SEARCH FOR THE MARROW

Olaf continues to dig for the holy grail, despite Valleygirl's threats to leave him if he doesn't quit. A homesick Orvil decides to return to the farm. Morley and Alfreda become passionate, but he has problems performing. Tofu figures out how to open the refrigerator door and gets the special cheesecake planned for Master's birthday party. Bertha rolls in the compost pile. Afro still cannot find his nylabone and suspects that Toto and Tabatha have stolen it, so he decides to destroy the Kleenex boxes and make it look like they did it. Sophia taunts Imelda by telling her that her framed pedigree is a fake.

DOGUE

fashion neckware

taste test RESULTS

Meet Our Panel...

Wally the Garbage Disposal

Chewy Chewmonger

Persnickety Snowflake

Items taste-tested:

	Wally the Garbage Disposal	Chewy Chewmonger	Persnickety Snowflake
BIG BAG O' BONES	Delicious & delectable!	OK, tastes like dog food.	Totally disgusting.
pure Bread	Lip-smacking good!	OK, tastes like dog food.	I'd rather starve.
Beggar's Choice	Absolutely fabulous!	OK, tastes like dog food.	Barely edible.
DOGIVA	Decadently scrumptious!	OK, tastes like dog food.	Well, maybe...

At the end of your tether?

Tired of annoying doors, impenetrable gates, frustrating fences, and daunting walls?

If artificial structures are blocking your road to roam, you need the **Great Escapes Video Series**. Thanks to the Clever Canines at **Great Escapes, Inc.**, any dog, regardless of background, breeding, brains, or training, can learn how to get around, under, over, and even through the most difficult obstacles—like magic! Escape your backyard blues and discover the world.

GREAT ESCAPES

Chain-link Fences Simplified

Order the complete 5-video set A steal at 795 Milk-Bones

Order the Great Escapes Video Series TODAY!

Video 1/Understanding Door Knobs (only 195 Milk-Bones*)

Video 2/Gate Crashing 1-2-3 (just 195 Milk-Bones*)

Video 3/Chain-link Fences Simplified (merely 195 Milk-Bones*)

Video 4/The Art of Burrowing Under (simply 195 Milk-Bones*)

Video 5/Making Invisible Fences Disappear (just 195 Milk-Bones*)

To order call 1-800-ESCAPE

* Please include two beef-flavored Jerky Snacks per video for pawing and shipping

iron dog winner!

Congratulations to SEBASTIAN BARKIN on winning the **2003 NATIONAL IRON DOG TRIATHLON!** The phenomenal canine athlete, a one-year-old, six-pound Pomeranian from Virginia, beat out an elite field of over 100 competitors in the grueling endurance contest comprised of a 3-mile open-water retrieval swim, followed by 100 consecutive fly ball laps and a 26-mile lure coursing run. Sebastian's victory was completely unexpected—thrilling the crowd of enthusiastic spectators. Asked how he felt about his performance, a panting Barkin said, "That was fun, can we do it again?" Retired Iron-Dog champion, Flash Pluton, had this to say: "Sebastian is one awesome dude! The rest of the pack never stood a chance." Among the favored competitors chasing Sebastian's tail were:

PEPPER HIGGINS, a champion Australian Shepherd from Scooby, Montana

COSMO DANIELS, an over-achieving Flat-coated Retriever from the Chesapeake Bay.

TONTO TADI, one of the fastest Ibizan hounds in the west.

THE 7 HABITS OF HIGHLY EFFECTIVE BEGGARS

BY MOOCH FILLMORE

Who says beggars can't be choosers? Effective begging can be your ticket onto a gravy train full of everything from hot dogs to holy mackerel, often offered right from your human's hand. Sounds like pie in the sky, you say? Then you need to bone up on your begging skills.

Here's some food for thought:

• Always use salami tactics—that is, take small steps, don't go hog wild.

• When offered a hand-out, never bite off more than you can chew.

• If you accidentally bite the hand that feeds you, drop it like a hot potato.

• Avoid eating your human out of house and home or you'll end up scraping the bottom of the barrel.

• Whenever the opportunity arises, DO take candy from a baby!

• When what's cooking makes your mouth water, try to keep from foaming at the mouth.

• Alternatively, if something smells fishy, or you encounter sour grapes, don't beef about it; sometimes that's just the way the cookie crumbles.

• And if that cookie happens to crumble on the floor, it's fair game.

Similarly, never let your human cry over spilt milk—lap it up immediately. If the Big Cheese tosses you a meager crumb of comfort, swallow your pride and don't make any bones about it; just wolf it down and beg the question, "More please?" Some other humans may try to convince your human that "human food" is bad for dogs. Doesn't that just take the cake! Those humans are full of beans—forbidden fruit tastes best! As long as you know which side your bread is buttered on, you can avoid bare bones and bad eggs.

Yes, life is a picnic; with effective begging habits, you can have your cake and eat it too!

THE 7 HABITS

1. SERVE NO WHINE BEFORE ITS TIME

Whining is the most basic begging strategy, but for it to be successful the timing and delivery of the whine is key. Imagine that your Mistress is sitting in front of the tube, force-feeding herself Cool Ranch Doritos from an industrial-sized bag. An inexperienced beggar would be inclined to let loose with a sudden, loud, high-pitched whine, which, in nine cases out of ten, will get that hound kicked out of the house before it gets a single hand-out. Try this instead: Cock your head cutely to one side, give an imploring look with wrinkled forehead and soulful eyes, then whine softly, questioningly. If no chips fall, sit back on your haunches, put your front paws together in an undeniable appeal, and increase the volume and tempo of the whine. As a last resort, pump up the volume to full staccato whine and jump frantically around the room until the Doritos spill onto the floor—or you get evicted from the premises.

2. BEING FED A LOT OF BALONEY, OR "WHAT? DOG FOOD AGAIN?"

When another bowl of dull, dry kibble is placed unceremoniously before you, sniff it disgustedly, sigh deeply, and look up at your Master as if to say, "Is this all there is, my friend?" Then follow him to the table and stare up at him, pointedly sniffing as he consumes his three-course meal. If your human has any compassion at all, with enough training he'll get the message and share some real food with you.

3. LET THE CHIPS FALL WHERE THEY MAY

Developing good Kitchen Patrol habits is fun and easy. When a human capable of opening the refrigerator or operating a can-opener enters the kitchen, stand ready for K.P. duty. Watch carefully and inhale any food morsel that hits the floor. Advanced beggars should strive to inhale morsels before they hit the floor. Be ecologically minded: Never allow leftovers go down the garbage disposal—insist on recycling them yourself; and always pre-rinse those dishes with your tongue before they go into the dishwasher.

And always remember to say "thank you" with a lick

continued on page 26

THE 7 HABITS

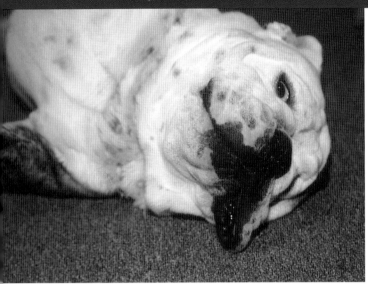

4. THE MILK OF HUMAN KINDNESS

Less active dogs will find this habit fits right in with their lethargic lifestyle. When your humans sit down to eat, sprawl out in the middle of the floor with your eyes half open and whimper pathetically. Your humans will be concerned that something is wrong with you and attempt to determine if the problem is gastrointestinal (a big word they learned from disgusting TV commercials) by offering you some of their lasagna. Sniff the proffered pasta with disinterest and (this is the hard part) try not to inhale it; remember, you are supposed to be out of sorts. Wait for your humans to gently stroke your tummy and coo encouraging words along the lines of, "Per favore, Geno, eat justa one leetle bite of ze pasta for Papa," then reward them by chewing the (INCREDIBLY MOUTH-WATERING!) lasagna slowly and deliberately. During breaks, as members of the family go off to get you more to eat, give their cheeks weak but grateful licks when they return. As they assess your gastrointestinal status with more bites of lasagna (and perhaps some crusty Italian bread!), act as though each successive mouthful is restoring you to health until you have successfully helped them polish off the meal.

5. TABLE MANNERS

This is especially effective at large dinner parties. Select the most gullible-looking guest—she will usually be a female. As the group sits down for dinner, lie down behind her chair without drawing attention to yourself. When your patsy excuses herself to "go powder her nose" (a behavior no Dog has yet been able to interpret) take a deep breath and, just as the back legs of her chair crash into your soft, vulnerable underbelly, let out a blood-curdling yelp. When all eyes are on you, limp around in circles, head down, ears back, tail clamped between your legs, whimpering softly. Give a few furtive looks over your shoulder, as if in anticipation of more abuse, and pant anxiously. This is all you should have to do to bring the guilty (and now embarrassed) guest to her knees to make sure you are "Okay?" Eyeing her plate, let her know that some of her pork tenderloin with mashed potatoes and gravy would speed up the healing process. With a little luck (and good acting skills) you might be able to milk your guest right through dessert!

AN IMPORTANT TIP: Do not forget which part of you is injured; humans (especially lawyer types) are sticklers for such details, and may catch on to your ruse if you suddenly start limping on the wrong leg. Also, don't overdo the pain and suffering—you don't want a visit to the vet.

6. EATING HUMBLE PIE

As demeaning as it may be, you should get into the habit of performing silly, unsolicited tricks whenever food is present. Humans are easily amused by spontaneous sit-ups, roll-overs, and paw shakes, and will usually reward such efforts. More novel tricks (such as sliding down the banister, or riding the skateboard) can be extremely lucrative. Remember: Perform only for edible rewards.

"A well-trained dog will make no attempt to share your lunch. He will just make you feel so guilty that you cannot enjoy it."
–Helen Thomson

7. A HARD NUT TO CRACK

Sending subliminal suggestions to your human while he or she is engaged in the all-consuming act of eating requires intense focus, imagery, and practice, so don't be discouraged if it doesn't work the first time. Start by positioning yourself so that you can establish eye contact with the food. Follow every fork-to-mouth movement as you telepathically send your human one or more of the following messages:

"I wonder how much of this pot roast The Dog could eat?"

"Wow, I'm so full I can't eat another bite of this pot roast! May as well give it to The Dog."

"What a great Dog! I think I'll give him the rest of my pot roast."

SUMMARY

Effective begging requires desire, patience, and regular practice of THE 7 HABITS OF HIGHLY EFFECTIVE BEGGARS. Study your human's feeding habits. Innovate and adapt your begging strategies. And always remember to say "thank you" with a lick: appreciation is almost as important as proper begging itself. Bone Appétit! 🐾

DISCLAIMER: The author is not liable, nor assumes any responsibility, for any pain or suffering experienced by any Dog who gets put on a diet due to unsightly weight gain brought about by following THE 7 HABITS OF HIGHLY EFFECTIVE BEGGARS program.

Unique de jour dining

Le Dumpster Restaurante

Reservations s'il vous plait 555-DUMP

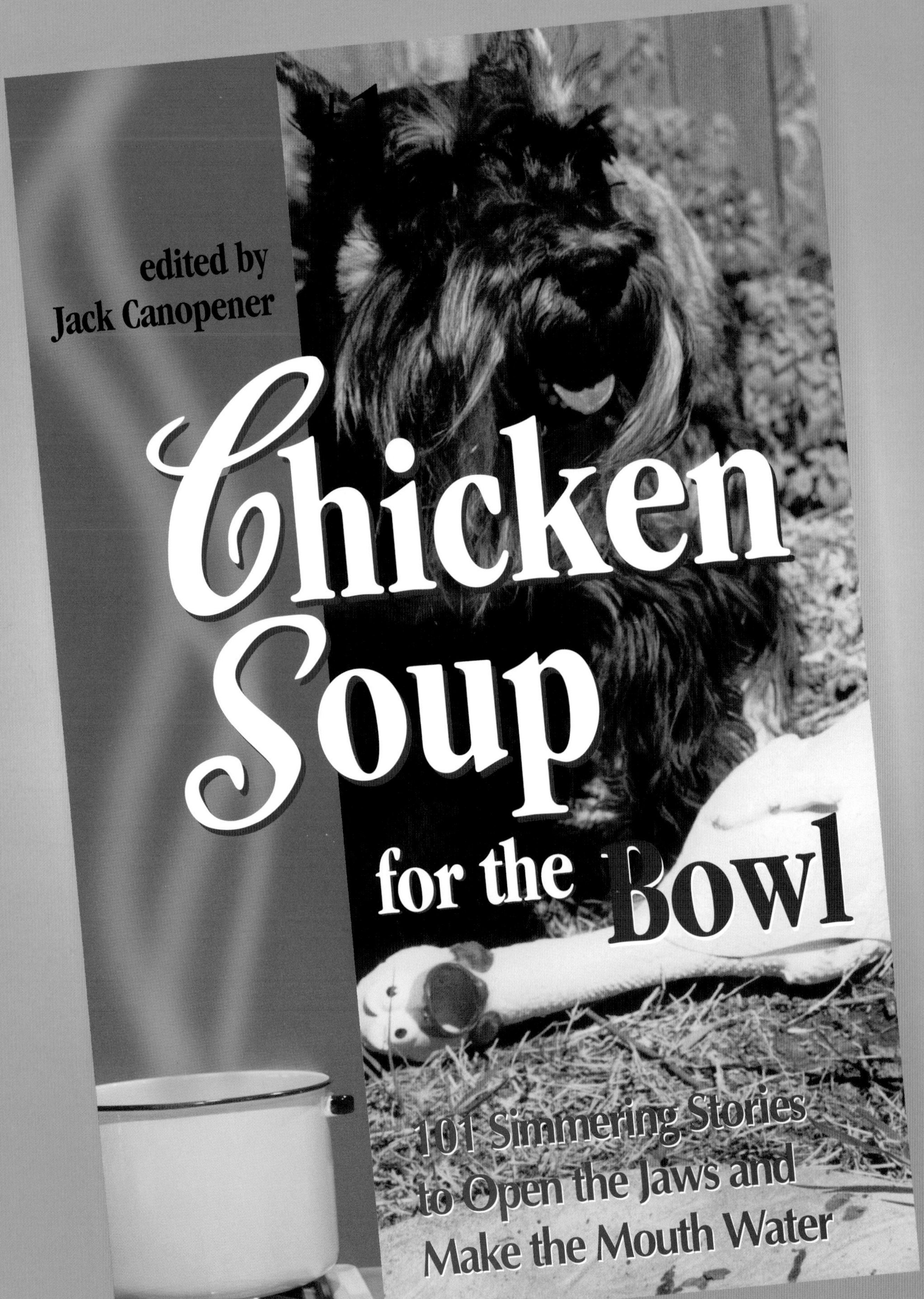

edited by
Jack Canopener

Chicken
Soup
for the Bowl

101 Simmering Stories
to Open the Jaws and
Make the Mouth Water

ONE OF MY FAVORITE THINGS

By Wolfgang Pug

I wish Sonia could have enjoyed this dish with me ... Wolf

Hearty Black Forest Roadkill
Marinated in Mud

This delicious entrée should be prepared in the autumn when fresh roadkill is plentiful and soil moisture and temperature are perfect for marinating. Radish or mustard greens bring out the natural juices. The pungent flavor of the finished roadkill is complemented by the subtle taste of the watercress, and the dried fall leaves add an unexpected crunchy texture. I like to serve this dish with an aged mash of fermented juniper berries.

1 fresh roadkill (squirrel, opossum, bunny
   or any other dead critter; avoid skunk)
Dark, loamy soil
Several gallons water
Dried leaves
Wild radish or mustard greens
Watercress
Wild leeks
Wild mushrooms (optional)

Have roadkill at "room" temperature. In dark, loamy soil dig a hole large enough for the entire carcass. Reserve excavated dirt. Wait for a rainstorm or the sprinkler system to fill the hole with water. Work dirt and water together until it is the consistency of drool; remove any roots, rocks or other impurities. Roll the roadkill in crushed dried leaves and wrap with a thin layer of wild radish or mustard greens. Carefully drop the roast into the marinating hole, breast side up. Cover with reserved dirt. Mark the hole well. Allow to marinate for one week or until it smells done. Take care when excavating the roadkill; it will be very tender. Arrange the carcass on a bed of watercress and garnish with wild leeks. Serve with fresh morels, truffles or shiitake mushrooms if available. Leftovers can be re-buried for up to four months. ***Bone Appétit!***

Serves 1 Mastiff, 3 Boxers, or 37 Chihuahuas.

g

groomingtail's

DOGS' LIFE readers' survey

Boss, head of our Marking and Advertising Department, wants to know more about you. So grab a pencil (#2) and fill out this short survey, or Boss will be really mad. Then send it to Boss at DOGS' LIFE magazine. And don't lie!

Pedigree
- ❏ Mixed breed
- ❏ Purebred
- ❏ Have no idea

Approximate age
- ❏ Hyper-pup
- ❏ Prime Time
- ❏ Gray around the muzzle

Occupation
- ❏ Professional Dog
- ❏ Lap Dog
- ❏ Unemployed Stray

Status
- ❏ Loner
- ❏ Lonely
- ❏ Spayed/Neutered
- ❏ Valuable Bitch/Stud

Level of education
- ❏ Un-trainable
- ❏ Sat through Basic Obedience nine times
- ❏ Canine Good Citizen
- ❏ Master's degree

Do you roll in smelly stuff?
- ❏ All the time
- ❏ Whenever I can get away with it
- ❏ Never appealed to me

Favorite vacation
- ❏ Ride in the car
- ❏ Club Shed
- ❏ Westminster Kennel Club

What type of collar do you wear?
- ❏ Chain mail choker
- ❏ Designer faux Jackal hide
- ❏ None, I live in a nudist colony

When on a walk, do you heel?
- ❏ Yes
- ❏ No
- ❏ Heal? Do I look like an M.D?

In the car, where do you ride?
- ❏ Driver's seat
- ❏ Shotgun
- ❏ Run around in the bed of the truck

Are you a Latchkey dog?
- ❏ Yes, and I can't figure out the *!#~ key!
- ❏ No, I have my very own doggie door

What's your favorite trick?
- ❏ Goosing my human just as she picks up her first cup of morning coffee
- ❏ Scooting across the oriental carpet during *Survivor*
- ❏ Counter surfing

Which do you regularly drink? (mark all that apply)
- ❏ Toilet water
- ❏ Firewater
- ❏ Bathwater

How often do you roam?
- ❏ Never
- ❏ Daily
- ❏ Only on the full moon

Do you like to dig?
- ❏ Yes, I am almost to China
- ❏ Depends on soil condition
- ❏ Only for a worthwhile bone

How far from home do you roam?
- ❏ I only leave my couch for emergencies
- ❏ Around the block
- ❏ As far as I can go without getting lost
- ❏ Until I am totally lost and my human has to come pick me up

What credit cards do you own?
- ❏ Master'sCard
- ❏ Visla Card
- ❏ American Excess

BY SMELLANY POST

Dog Park Etiquette

The biggest "NO-NO!" at a dog park is picking a dog fight.

Planning to visit a dog park but have never been off-leash before? There's more to it than turning a deaf ear to your human and running your tail off. Yes, Rover, there are rules of etiquette you need to know before leaping into the furry fray with all four paws.

First off: sniffing. As you enter the park every dog within olfactory range will approach (some at top speed) to "greet you," i.e., to sniff and be sniffed. If your sniffing style has gotten you into trouble, or you just want to brush up on your manners, I recommend you read, *Sniff, But Don't Miff* by Missy Manners, or attend a sniffing etiquette class at Chauncy's Charm School.

This, naturally, brings me to the topic of sex. The freedom of being leash-less in the presence of so many new and interesting dogs can be intoxicating, especially for the recently initiated. Combine this with some enthusiastic and amorous sniffing and seductive bow plays, and you can easily find yourself engaged in carnal activities. While this is not a problem for us dogs, it is often considered to be a source of embarrassment for our humans. After witnessing many a dog's amorous gestures being met with, shall we say, a heavy hand, I strongly recommend that, should you decide to engage a little playmate, you keep a sharp eye out for swinging newspapers.

While we're on the subject of humans, let me just remind you that they, as a rule, do not enjoy being jumped upon, especially when wearing "good clothes." That said, I must confess that I can rarely resist the opportunity. I prepare for the event by taking a quick dip in the mud puddle (if one is not available, a run through dew-soaked grass will do) followed by a roll in the dust. Then, drooling like an idiot, and wearing that look of, "Oh, boy, oh boy! I'm just SO happy to see you!" I bound straight for the most immaculately dressed human available, veering off at the last second as they cringe into a protective fetal position. The look on their face is priceless. Don't get

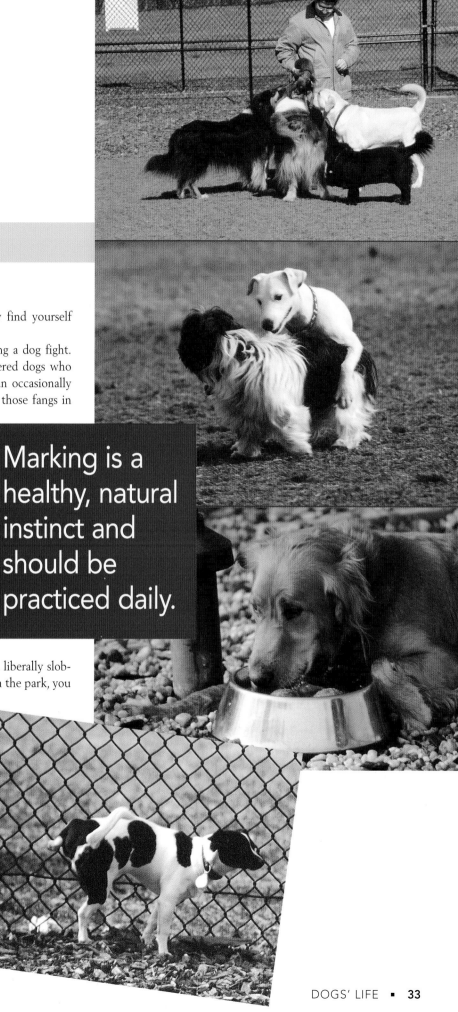

carried away with this game though, or you may find yourself being carried out of the park.

The biggest "NO-NO!" at a dog park is picking a dog fight. Fortunately, fighting is rare among the well-mannered dogs who frequent these parks; however, a little ruff play can occasionally turn nasty. Leave your alpha-ego at the gate, keep those fangs in check, and you shouldn't stir up any trouble.

A lot of humans have a water fetish, both for themselves and for us dogs. A well-equipped dog park will have plenty of fresh water available—a good thing because dog park play is thirsty business. Do take advantage of the water bowls, but do not hog them or use them to wash off your tennis balls, and please, please, do not pee in them once you have drunk your fill: You would not believe how many rude dogs I have seen doing such things in the common bowl!

Humans love to recycle their dogs' old used toys, and a well-equipped dog park will have many toys lying about. At the better parks the toys will be dirty, worn, well-chewed and liberally slobbered on, enhancing their desirability. Depending on the park, you can expect to find Frisbees, tennis balls, tug-of-war toys, soccer balls, Kongs, and more. Enjoy these, play all you want, just don't hog any toy for too long—unless no one else wants it—and, in that case, abandon it for something everyone else does find interesting.

A final word: marking. Marking is a healthy, natural instinct and it should be practiced daily. But no matter how fanatically you mark the dog park, it will never become your personal territory. Once you accept this basic fact you'll have much more time to devote to romping, digging, panting, and playing with your own kind. 🐾

> Marking is a healthy, natural instinct and should be practiced daily.

GUARANTEED

Shar-Pei
WRINKLE-CREME
by CoverGirrrlll

Are you a Good Dog... ...or a Bad Dog?

Take this DOGS' LIFE Whiz Quiz and find out

1. Your master comes home from a hellish day of work. You:

❑ A Greet him at the door with his slippers,
a dry martini and a plate of pigs' ears.

❑ B Give a bark or two from your bed just to
let him know you are home.

❑ C Ignore him until after you have inspected
his clothes then let him know you are hungry,
bored and in need of a walk.

2. Your mistress just burned another batch of cookies and is about to have a nervous breakdown. You:

❑ A Salivate profusely, and beg enthusiastically
for burnt offerings.

❑ B Sniff the acrid air with distaste and head outside.

❑ C Throw up on the oriental carpet.

3. The children are having a sleepover and decide to put curlers in your fur, dress you up like Prom Barbie and dance you around the room on your hind paws. You:

❑ A Good-naturedly put up with them (despite broken nails,
a dislocated shoulder and bald patches) then bring out
your own vintage Barbie collection to share with them.

❑ B Yelp, struggle free and hide under the bed.

❑ C Bite one of the obnoxious brats on the nose then
whiz on her father's wingtips when he comes to get her.

4. Your mistress is hosting her parents' golden wedding anniversary; food is everywhere and the guests are getting tipsy. You:

❑ A Answer the door, serve the canapés, clean up
and volunteer to be the Designated Driver.

❑ B Work the crowd with agility and charm,
enjoying every tidbit.

❑ C Help yourself to the liver paté and boldly
sniff every crotch in the room.

5. Master and Mistress are in bed, doing "it." You:

❑ A Discretely leave the room hanging out the
"Do Not Disturb" sign as you go.

❑ B Sit attentively on the end of the bed and stare.

❑ C Jump under the covers and propose a *menage-a-trois*.

6. It is very late. Everyone is fast asleep. You hear an intruder breaking into the house. You:

❑ A Call 911, tackle the burglar and hold him
by his jugular until the cops arrive.

❑ B Bark like Rin Tin Tin until you actually see
the burglar, then hide behind Master.

❑ C Hide under the bed as quick as you can.

7. While driving with your elderly master in an unfamiliar part of town you become aware that he is lost. You:

❑ A Open the glove box, pull out the appropriate map,
and make intelligent whining sounds.

❑ B Hang your head out the window and enjoy
the new smells.

❑ C Bark loudly in his ear to get him to pull over
and then jump out and have casual sex with
the first dog you come across.

HOW YOU SCORED:

Mostly C's: Oh, You Bad Dog! What can we say, you just do as you please, right?

Mostly B's: A Dog's Dog! While your owner might wish that you were more Lassie-like, you are popular among your fellow canines for having your priorities in order.

Mostly A's: Since no doggy could be this good we figure that you must have cheated! And that makes you a Sneaky Dog.

DOGS' LIFE Calendar

1 Mark yard	**2** Break in Master's new running shoes	**3** Cruise soup kitchens	**4** Take squirrel out for lunch	**5** Age bones	**6** Bury bones	**7** Search for bones
8 Try to forget about bones by cleaning out refrigerator	**9** Clean private parts	**10** Inspect food dish for leaks	**11** Augment compost pile	**12** Full moon: Howl and run amok	**13** Raid downtown dumpsters	**14** Find out what "Hair of the Dog" really means
15 Bury hatchet	**16** Teach cat how to swim	**17** Water grass and kill emergent weeds	**18** Get laundry down from clothesline	**19** Collect tennis balls from neighbor's court	**20** Shop around for intriguing and pungent scent to wear	**21** Nap day
22 Play practical joke on cat	**23** Re-create pedigree	**24** Clean kitchen floor	**25** Artfully arrange toys throughout the house	**26** Dig up bulbs	**27** Study herding book	**28** Finish toilet paper maché sculpture
29 Check p-mail	**30** Excavate new flowerbed	**31** Mark time				

NEW! FROM FRISE PRESS...

Pierre du Pea

The Ultimate Guide

FIRE HYDRANTS of France

FIRE HYDRANTS OF FRANCE: THE ULTIMATE GUIDE
by Pierre du Pea

Even if you never get to France, this beautiful, fully revised edition of FIRE HYDRANTS OF FRANCE, by Pierre du Pea, the world's most renowned hydrant connoisseur, is a must for the sophisticated Dog's library.

FIRE HYDRANTS OF FRANCE features page after exciting page of sepia tone photos, fragrant descriptions, well-marked maps, and suggested tour routes. Plus, history comes alive with Pierre's translations of important messages left by famous Dogs at French hydrants: Discover the secret messages that were passed between Napoleon's Toy Poodle, Neapolitan, and Wellington's Bloodhounds.

FOR THE FINEST IN CREATURE COMFORTS

BEG FOR

BARKALOUNGER

*Dog House
of the Month*

Adrift
in the Lap
of Luxury

BY RHODA GNAWBERG
PHOTOGRAPHED BY
ANSEL LEIBOVITZ

> "…I HAD A LARGE STOCK OF
> DRIFTWOOD, SO I STARTED
> EXPERIMENTING WITH IT
> AS A BUILDING MATERIAL."

I t is easy to be fooled by the unimposing structure perched above the high tide line on a secluded and rugged beach in the Gulf of Alaska. At first glance it appears to be merely an abandoned wooden teepee ravaged by the wind and rain. Closer inspection, however, reveals a Dog house of truly sublime style and functionality.

When Chester Goldenrod, a seasoned driftwood importer from Homer, Alaska, met the love of his life and decided to settle down, he was told, unequivocally, that he would need to provide more than a stamped-down patch of sea oats in which to raise his new family. "My mate, Goldie, made it clear that she expected a real roof, not a ruff, over her and the puppies' heads. I'd never built a Dog house before, but I had a large stock of driftwood, so I started experimenting with it as a building material."

Chester discovered that aside from being a valuable trade commodity, driftwood is an ideal construction medium for the beach environment. "It's lightweight, easy to work

Adrift (continued from page 9)

with, and abundant. And if rations get low you can always chew on the walls," he explains, as he leads us through the portico.

The first thing we notice is that the entire structure is wonderfully devoid of doors, a design feature that allows unin-

Goldie relaxing at the beach

hibited egress and lets the music of the surf play freely throughout. In addition to providing stunning 360-degree views (which are ideal for bird hunting), the circular floor plan is ergonomically designed for curling up against the walls without having to contend with awkward corners. The inte-

rior walls, like the exterior walls, are wonderfully free of frills, allowing the natural rawness of the driftwood to stand out. Besides driftwood, the house is composed of stone and sand, materials chosen for their earthy colors and organic feel. Upstairs the lighting is purely natural: the sun by day, the stars and moon by night.

Because the house is exposed to the vagaries of wind, rain, sun, and sea birds, Chester wisely buries his most prized possessions below ground. A spiral staircase, reflecting the teepee's round design, leads down to the focal point of the family den—a massive circular stone fireplace adorned with exquisite 16th century tapestries depicting fox hunting scenes. Grouped around the fireplace are overstuffed leather sofas and club chairs. Plush oriental carpets, collected from around the world, cover the soft sand-based flooring in an elegantly haphazard fashion. This is truly a room to roll over and nap in. Although not palatial in size, the house is roomy enough for a family of 17, and can even accommodate unexpected stray weekend house guests.

Adjacent to the den is the Provincial-inspired kitchen, rich with the scent of raw meat. Here we find Goldie at work filling water bowls from the paw-operated water cooler. The func-

tional yet free-spirited room is also equipped with floor-level counters and a walk-in refrigerator. Pedigreed dinner guests are offered gourmet treats served on fine bone china Dog dishes.

Chester's office is efficient yet friendly, containing all the accoutrements emblematic of a successful white-collar Dog. The family photographs and personal travel souvenirs render a warm and fuzzy feel to the room. "This is my private space," says Chester. "Whenever I feel low, or there's a thunderstorm outside, I come down here and curl up with my favorite chunk of driftwood."

The nursery is currently under construction. "I'm still trying to decide whether to go with the Snoopy theme or Lady and The Tramp," explains Goldie. Her exclusive San Francisco decorating team is coordinating the colors and textures of the whelping, teething and paper-training areas.

HIS and HERS hydrants

When asked what they enjoy most about their Dog house, the couple leads us straight to the Moorish-style master bathroom. "Actually, Goldie did most of the decorating herself," Chester boasts. Clearly, no expense was spared in this large and elegant space. It is equipped with two superbly restored antique fire hydrants (one English and one French) discovered by the newlyweds at a flea market, a bone-shaped heated lap pool, and a custom-made digging pit filled with sand imported from Barking Sands Beach on the island of Kauai.

It would appear that Chester and his bride have truly created a very special place in which to raise their first litter. "We want our pups to gain an appreciation for form and function as well as style and aesthetics," they say. The puppies are due next month. 🐾

"A door is what a dog is perpetually on the wrong side of."
—Ogden Nash

SEE THE BRITISH COUNTRYSIDE IN CLASSIC DOGGY-STYLE!

OFF THE BEATEN PATH

BOOK YOUR NEXT ENGLISH HOLIDAY WITH THE FINEST!
"OFF THE BEATEN PATH" AUTO-DOGGY TOURS

- Sniff the very bog where the Hounds of the Baskervilles roamed •
- Enjoy a private audience with the Queen's Welsh Corgis •
- Visit the famous Dog Collar Museum in Leeds Castle •
- Watch an authentic, fast-paced country fox hunt •
- Swim in a real medieval moat •

CALL 1-800-OFBEAT FOR RESERVATIONS

We'll help you put the WAG back in your walk!

A·T·T·I·T·U·D·E

"Not a shred of evidence exists in favor
of the idea that life is serious."
—Brendan Gill

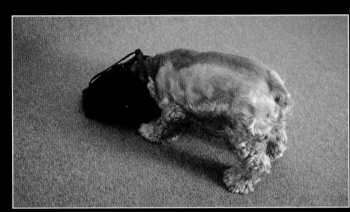

P·E·R·S·I·S·T·E·N·C·E

"To see what is in front of one's nose requires a constant struggle."
—George Orwell

MUTTIVATIONAL POSTERS
· FROM DOGMA-TEASERS INC. ·

These captivating posters, with their thoughtful and inspiring quotes
are perfect for rousing lazier members of the pack into high gear.
They make marvelous gifts, and are just the thing to perk up a
colorless crate or dull doghouse.

As usual, all images are available in the following:

Poster in raw wood-frame *(perfect for hi-fiber chewing)*   39.99 Milk-Bones
Poster un-framed *(ideal for easier chewing)*   29.99 Milk-Bones
Greeting Cards 6-pack *(excellent for a quick chew)*   9.99 Milk-Bones

A·D·V·E·N·T·U·R·E

"Keep trying. Stay humble. Trust your instincts.
Most importantly, ACT. When you come to a
fork in the road, take it."
—Yogi Berra

F·R·I·E·N·D·S·H·I·P

"'Stay' is a charming word in a friend's vocabulary."
—Bronson Alcott

ask:
an Australian Shepherd

BY OZZY DRIVER

Dear Ozzy,

My master was fired from Pie Face Pizza three weeks ago. He worked for them for over 22 years and was their best delivery guy. He loved that job, and so did I; I got to ride along most nights, and we always had plenty of Carnivore's Choice Supreme in the fridge. Now, without meaningful employment, all he does is sit in front of the TV and play with his remote. Why doesn't he go look for another job at Mona Pizza, or The Steaming Tower of Pizza, or even ask the jerk at Pie Face for his old job back? I need a pepperoni fix!

Hungry in Hanover

Dear Hungry,

Competitive sheep herding might look easy to the uninitiated, and that's because professional shepherds, like me, practice for hours on end to refine their skills. When you work a herd from dawn to dusk, cutting and culling and running

along the backs of the stupid sheep, you are dog tired at the end of the day. Herding is nearly as demanding mentally as it is physically. You must pay close attention to the man's hand and whistle signals, and try not to get all pissed off when he screws up. You also have to keep your eye on the damn sheep and anticipate their every move—some of them can be pretty cagey. And, hardest of all, you have to nip their heels but not draw blood or go totally berserk and open up their jugular vein. You should ask yourself if you really have what it takes to be a shepherd; it's not for every dog after all.

Dear Ozzy,

After a number of disastrous relationships with a variety of purebred and mixed breed dogs, I have finally found the right male for me. He's soft and loveable and he says he loves me unconditionally. He's a Prince; in fact, that's even his name. But after dating all those other vicious jerks, I find that I'm suspicious of him: I follow him wherever he goes, I read his private scent marks, I even checked that his rabies tag was up to date. I don't want to mess up the only good relationship I've had so far. How do I handle my distrust?

—In Love in Louisville

Dear In Love,

The single most important aspect in being a successful shepherd is knowing how to give sheep "the eye." Sheep will not respect or obey you unless you can intimidate them by capturing and holding their gaze instantly. Practice by staring at yourself in the mirror for as long as possible. If you experience dry-eye use Visine or a similar product. Always give the eye to the most stubborn sheep: once you have him under control the rest will follow. You will rarely hear a superior shepherd bark at his herd: all he needs to do is give good eye.

Dear Ozzy,

Supposedly I was "fixed," you know, spayed, when I was younger, but I'm pretty sure I'm pregnant. I'm worried because I don't know who the father is. It could be Hershey, the lab across the street, or it might be Tonka, the English Toy spaniel from the park, or, my worst fear, it may be Psycho, the stray Pit Bull from Detroit. If it is Psycho, I could end up with a litter of little Cujos on my paws! Is there any way I can find out who the father is?

—Pregnant and Puzzled in Pokipsie

Dear Pregnant and Puzzled,

If you are ever separated from your flock of sheep, don't panic. Panic will only get you overly excited and cause you to make more mistakes. Stay calm and look for something else to herd: dust bunnies, falling leaves, ants, even blades of grass. Rely on your training and instincts and you'll be OK.

OZZY DRIVER *is an award-winning shepherd and herding consultant. His syndicated monthly column appears courtesy of* The Shepherd Times.

Pookie's *diary*

Saturday morning

This early-morning exercise thing is wicked! "Tally-ho Pookie! Time for our Morning Walkies!" she coos, hauling me out the door. Wherever did she get an Aerobics For Oldies Kit anyway? And what makes Dotty think I want to be her workout buddy? Can't she see I absolutely loathe physical exertion? I'm the laughingstock of the neighborhood, trudging down the lane behind her capaciously swaying rear end. On top of all that, I need a pedicure.

Sunday...sometime...

Torture! Dotty left the house this morning with the telly tuned to that stupid show, "Chick Chat." Full volume, too! Had to un-stuff a few pillows to preserve my sanity. Dotty came home and gave me the usual lecture: "Oh-oh, my Pookie-wookie's been a naughty boy again, hasn't he?" Tough! That old widower from across the street is coming over for dinner tonight and Dotty-Wotty is making my favorite—Steak & Kidney Pie. Yip-yip-yip-yip-yip!

Monday afternoon

Thank Dog for bridge days! Dotty told the divine Mrs. Reed that I was on a diet and not to feed me any more bridge mix—but she snuck me some whenever Dotty stared down dumbly at her cards. Must have been some night last night. I found the old widower's hairpiece behind the sofa and dragged it out to show the bridge club. Looks a bit like a roadkill. Not much flavor though.

Tuesday evening

Nearly broke that damned swizzle stick the vet stuck up my bum this morning! Well he'd have squirmed too if somebody did that to his hind end. Dotty attempted to make it up to me by letting me lie in her ample lap and watch Lassie re-runs. Does she have to interrupt all the good parts saying things like, "Oh, look Pookie-wookie, Lassie is telling Timmy's daddy that Timmy fell down the well; he's such a smart dog!" Honestly, that dog is a lot smarter than Timmy. Why don't his parents cap that well, anyway?

Wednesday afternoon

Was served that stale, tasteless, diet dog food again today. And all because that vermin who calls himself a vet thinks I've gone a bit too thick round the middle. Had an unexpected visit from that busybody Mrs. Bland this morning. She very undiplomatically accused me of fathering those ugly, whining puppies that mutt of hers produced. Ridiculous! I wouldn't have mounted that homely bitch if she'd begged me. Some humans will say anything to save face.

Thursday evening

I was looking forward to our weekly trip to the grocery store this morning until Dot strapped me into that new Safe Pooch seat belt contraption she bought from the shopping network. It's bad enough that I can't jump back and forth in the car barking at passing dogs, but did she have to buy a hot-pink harness? Makes me look such a pansy. Wonder how long it will take me to chew through the bloody thing.

Friday morning

Getting really tired of telling Dotty to leave the back door open. It is summer after all. Good news: Dot is going away with the old widower for the week-end, which means that Taffy from Pampered-Pet Sitters will be staying with me. She's such a pushover. Bye-bye diet dog food! Hey, is that another vacu-

um cleaner salesman coming up the walk? Maybe I can scare the stuffing out of him. Arrrrrrrrfff! 🐾

b o x e r s

They bring out the best in any breed.

By SheBear de la Laisse
Illustrated by Dennis Crawford

leash-less
in Seattle

"She loves you, yeah, yeah, yeah.
She loves you..."

BUUZZZZZ!

"And now, here's Freeway Freddy with your
KSEA 6 a.m. traffic report. Hey, how's
that commute going this morning,
Freddy Boy?"

"Well, Dick, in a word, it's NOT!"

**"...yeah, yeah, yeah. She loves you, yeah, yeah,
yeah, yeaaaaaah."**

BUUZZZZZZZZZZZ!!!

Being jarred out of a sound sleep by the discordance of three competing
alarm clocks is one of the hazards of living with Elise. Fortunately for both of us,
her job as a freelance artist lets her set her own schedule and she rarely gets up
before the crack of noon. This morning though, she had an early breakfast meeting with a client, so she set the trio of alarms last night.

The cacophony itself never has an effect on Elise's slumber—she could
sleep through an asteroid landing in our living room. I realized long ago that the
true purpose of the alarms is to wake me up so that I can, in turn, wake her up.
I accomplish this by standing on her chest, barking hysterically, and licking her
nose as if it were a marrow bone. It's the only way to get her out of the sack!

Despite the sun streaming in the windows on this lovely midsummer
morning, Elise was even more sloth-like than usual: burrowing under the
covers, covering her head with the pillow, and making low grum-
bling noises. She has been uncharacteristically mopey, forgetful

and listless recently. Frankly, I believe her torpor is due to a stagnant love life. Unlike me, Elise doesn't find it rewarding to jump into a relationship with whatever interesting-smelling male crosses her path, and it's been a while since she's had a special someone in her life. Well, except for me, of course—SheBear, Elise's best friend and a most delightful Schipperke, if I do say so myself.

Anyway, it was not without concern that I watched her grope about our little houseboat, eyes half open (like mine were when I was still working the milk line as a pup), put her clothes on inside-out, wrestle with her hair then shove it under a hat, and search frantically for sunglasses that hung on a string around her neck. Somehow, she got herself and her portfolios together, gave me a kiss, grabbed a banana, and ran out the door, across the patio and out the gate, muttering something about being "…on time for once…." She was halfway down the pier when I noticed that the latch on our patio gate was broken. Scampering through my doggie door I went to investigate: sure enough, freedom was mine!

Now, I'm a pretty well behaved little dog (I even have my Master's degree in Basic Obedience), but I'd never been out for a walk on my own before, and the thought of spending the entire day leash-less in Seattle was, quite simply, irresistible. Feeling just the barest twinge of guilt, I watched for Elise's car to clatter out of sight before nudging the gate open and "Schipping out," so to speak. Oh, I did dash back inside to leave a note of shredded toilet paper saying that I would definitely be home for dinner; after all, I'm not completely irresponsible.

My neighbor, Amadeus (a Miniature Pinscher with a big crush on me), was sitting on his tidy little porch waiting, as he does every morning, to bark pointlessly at the paperboy. Amus (I call him that because it invariably sets him off) greeted me with his usual, "Hey, SheBear, you sexy little fox! How about a roll in the hay?" I scampered by, saying, "Not today, Amus, I'm headed for far more interesting adventures than that…." Poor fellow, he got himself all wound up again, turning those fast, tight little circles of his and barking out his high-pitched frustration.

We live in a great neighborhood full of quaint and quirky eateries. Famished, my first stop was my favorite outdoor café. Wearing my cutest expression, I persuaded a young woman to share her ham and egg croissant with me—so much tastier than that vegetarian stuff Elise feeds me. There's a certain satisfaction in begging food off of a perfect stranger; must be the hunter instinct.

Hunger satiated, at least temporarily, I wandered over to sniff the statue Elise calls, "Waiting for the Interurban."

I have no idea why; they might just as well have named it "Waiting for Godog." It's a group of humans and a little dog that—rumor has it—has a human's face. This I wanted to see for myself, as countless leash-bound walks had never allowed me a thorough inspection. Closer scrutiny confirmed that the sculptor had, indeed, given the canine the face of a biped—complete with beard! I didn't know whether to be insulted or flattered. I tell you, humans never cease to amaze me.

The sight of such a strange creature, mixed with the exotic scents of the Woodland Park Zoo, put me in a safari mood. (That only humans are allowed to visit the zoo is beyond me; dogs have just as much, if not more, interest in wild animals!) One time last spring, Elise smuggled me inside in her backpack and showed me giraffes, monkeys and bears before an obstinate zoo-keeper ran us out. What I really wanted to visit were the Big Cats I'd seen on *Animal Planet*. I wanted to know why they called them "Big Cats"—they didn't look so big on the TV. So, their den was my destination!

Sneaking into the zoo was a cinch once the busload of noisy first-graders arrived. As the kiddies were herded through the gate, I simply wandered into the middle of the unruly pack and, hidden by their scurrying little feet, trotted inside. Once in, I took cover in the bushes, dashing stealthily from shrub to shrub (like Secret Agent Dog!) until I picked up the unmistakable scent of kitty litter. It led me to a large enclosure where several kitties were lounging lazily in the sun. I was too far away to see just how big they were, so I squeezed between a narrow opening in the fence and trotted over for a better look.

As I approached, one of the cats flicked her tail and, purely out of habit, I began barking. "Arf-Arf! Arf-Arf! Arf!!" Another opened his eyes and looked straight at me. "Arf…Arf?" I said, losing some of my confidence as he stood, stretched, and yawned wide—revealing a mouthful of enormous fangs. "Oh *@#!*," I thought. "That really IS a BIG Cat!" I was somewhat dismayed (as in totally panic-stricken) that my most intimidating "Arf-Arfs" were not having the desired effect, that is to say the cats were not fleeing in terror. All I could do was stand there, frozen in place like the little dog in the Interurban statue, watching the enormous paws pad silently my way, the long tail casually swishing from side to side.

When we were, as Elise would say, up close and personal, I offered, in my most friendly little yip, "SO sorry to disturb you, Mr. Big Cat. I was looking for the hyenas—you know, those nasty little dog-like creatures with the funky teeth? My, your teeth aren't funky at all, are they?

Guess you brush, huh? Well, they are certainly very big and white and sharp-looking teeth, I must say. You know, I'd really love to hang around and discuss dentistry with you, but I absolutely must be running."

The Big Cat licked his chops and growled low—Darth Vader-ishly—"Hmmm, you yap too much...but you smell interesting. What flavor are you?"

"Actually," I said in a hurry, " I have no taste and no flavor either! And I'm tough and stringy, too."

He considered that for a moment, then opened his mouth to reveal those formidable fangs again. The smelly, hot roar he let out nearly blew me head over tail, and boy, did it get me moving.

"Nice meeting you, Mr. Cat," I squeaked, sprinting for the fence.

There are advantages to being small—among them speed, agility, and the ability to fit through tight spaces, all of which come in handy when being pursued by hungry tigers.

Ahh, sweet freedom! Out of the tiger's den, I made a bee-line for the exit, eluding a couple of excited zoo-keepers before escaping the zoo entirely. All I wanted now was some civilized Canine companionship, and I knew just where to find it: the off-leash area of the park where Elise and I come on weekends to play and socialize. My heart rate had returned to normal by the time I arrived, but it picked up again once I saw the agility class in progress.

A group of novice pups (with more energy than ability) were trying to follow the mixed-up signals of their human trainers. What the pups clearly needed was a demonstration by a pro. So I ran onto the course and displayed the proper techniques for clearing the hurdles, running the tunnels, weaving the poles, jumping the rings, and working the seesaw (I just love the seesaw). The applause was overwhelming (I also love applause). The pups wanted me to stick around and show them

some more—and, I must say, I was tempted to stay and flirt with that handsome blue-eyed Aussie—but I felt like a swim, and ran off to nearby Green Lake instead.

The sun was shining bright, warming the sand as I swam a few relaxing laps. Then, ready for a nap, I circled the requisite three times before curling up on the shore, and fell into a wonderful dream of puppy-hood: Ma was fussing over my litter-mates and I, licking us and hauling us around by the scruffs of our necks. I was just settling in for some nice warm milk...when I awoke to find myself sucking on a twig. Lying around like this was tempting, but I had things to do, doggies to meet, and places to go—among them the University of Washington where something is always happening. So I yawned and stretched, and trotted off to campus.

What joy! A rowdy game of Frisbee on the U. of W. Athletic Field! I don't want to brag, but I am a whiz at the sport, so I joined in, played left field, and caught the errant throws. I also managed to talk the guys out of a bag of potato chips before they had to "split for class," whatever that means. I just hope it isn't painful.

Game over, I wandered off to sniff the p-mail messages on the trashcans: one read, "Middle-aged mongrel seeking youthful, uninhibited playmate, flea collar a must." Oh brother! Another said, "For great scraps, beg at Joe's." There were several messages about it being a bumper year for squirrels in nearby Volunteer Park, and I figured I might as well check it out.

I was hardly inside the park before a plump little squirrel was lined up in my sights. There I was, primed and ready to lunge, when a cocky Spaniel came yapping up behind me, his intentions obvious. I would have been miffed at his bad timing had he not been wearing the most alluring scent; I think it was that new cologne, *d'animal*! We were sniffing each other excitedly when his human caught hold and yanked him roughly away, muttering something about nasty little beasts. Good grief, what a prude!

Needless to say, the human intrusion also sent the squirrel flying, leaving me doubly frustrated, and feeling like another nap.

It took only a few minutes to scope out the Bed & Breakfasts in the nearby neighborhood. I selected one with an open-door policy, sauntered in and made myself right at home on a supremely comfortable velvet sofa in the parlor. I was asleep in a flash and dreaming that I was riding a great big barge containing French Milk-Bones through the canals of Belgium, my ancestral home. I was the Top Dog in charge of rodent control—sniffing out and running fat rats off the barge to drown. The dream was just getting exciting when a terrible CRASH brought me back to reality.

A matronly woman wearing a most inhospitable expression loomed over me, her eyes bulging and darting between me and the remains of a tea service now strewn across the hardwood flooring and splattered all over an oriental carpet. The scent of milk and tea leaves hung in the air, and I could have really gone for one of those crumpets had the woman not started sputtering a slew of offensive remarks. I got the distinct impression that she felt I was somehow to blame for her clumsiness! No point in arguing with this one, though; better to scamper out of there like Goldilocks before Mama Bear could nab me.

I ran full out for ten blocks before stopping to catch my breath; when I did, a pack of kids ran past me, yelling and chasing a big white truck. Never one to pass up a good car chase, I joined in, barking enthusiastically. The truck pulled over to the side of the road immediately, no doubt intimidated by my pursuit. My smugness dissolved, however, the instant I saw the driver: dressed all in white, he looked just like a vet, a sight that elicited

unpleasant visions of sharp needles and cold probes. I kept my distance, ready to run should he come after me waving one of those nasty thermometer things, so I was astonished when he started handing out ice cream bars to the eager little mob of tots. Apparently, his truck was full of the frozen stuff!

Despite my phobia of white coats, I couldn't resist when he knelt down, pulled off the cover of a cup of vanilla ice cream and held it out to me. White Coat held the treat for me until I had licked it clean, then he patted me on the head, got back into his truck, and drove off—not unlike Santa! His truck didn't have any jingle bells, but it did play some terribly distorted music as it lumbered down the street.

Fortified by the creamy confection, I headed south on Broadway through a bohemian neighborhood full of some truly bizarre human beings. Now, Elise and her friends sometimes dress up in strange outfits (most notably on Halloween and New Year's Eve), but they never look as peculiar as the Broadway beings. Some of them wore leather collars studded with spikes just like the ones the junkyard dogs wear. Some sported hair that had clearly been blow-dried in a lightning storm. More than a few had rings dangling from their noses, belly buttons, and even their tongues. I thought maybe the rings were there for their owners to clip their leashes to—humans can be so peculiar! Most were friendly enough, though. One girl (I think it was a girl, anyway) got down on her hands and knees, gave me a pet, and read my tag. "SheBear? SheBear! Are you really a bear, SheBear?" she giggled idiotically. "No," I yipped, "I'm a Komodo dragon." Sigh! They all ask that. Time to move on.

I quickly discovered that vertically challenged dogs like me have to be careful negotiating the busier streets of this city. That's because Seattle motorists pride themselves on their ability to multi-task: while driving their cars they also drink low-fat lattès, read newspapers, chat on cell-phones, feed babies, apply makeup, and Dog knows what else. So there I was, minding my own business in the middle of the crosswalk, and a Hummer—that I think was being driven by two wild and crazy Weimaraners—came careening out of nowhere, nearly making roadkill out of me! As they sped away, I barked after them, "Hey, you wild and crazy Weimers, why don't you slow down and smell the intersections?" I don't think they even heard me.

Sticking to the sidewalk after that four-wheeled encounter, I managed to make my way to the tourist mecca of Pioneer Square, where I decided on a self-guided walking tour of the local fire hydrants. My interest was piqued by a particularly large hydrant on which a Great Dane, named Zeus, had left an intriguing poem. I was so engrossed in his vivid description of the bouquet of his true love's ear (at least I think it was "ear") that I never even saw the Animal Control van.

Had the goon been a tad quicker with that capture device of his I would have ended up in the pound, and with my day just beginning! I couldn't help feeling that this was no way for a city that claims to love dogs to treat its canine citizens. It made me wish (not for the first time) that I could communicate certain concepts to humans, such as: "Not all leash-less dogs are unwanted strays! Indeed, many are fully licensed, legitimate pets, just out for a little fresh air and exploration." However, my immediate concern was distancing myself from the un-civil servant. Without looking back, I ran like a Greyhound in heat, straight to Pike Place Market, ducked inside, and waited for my breath to catch up with me.

Having determined that I had successfully eluded my most recent pursuer, I relaxed a little and visited my favorite food vendors. Elise and I come to Pike Place all the time to buy fish, flowers and vegetables, so I know almost everyone. One of the fishmongers spotted me and tossed me a delightful appetizer of salmon sashimi. Tasty! I watched the fish guys throw whole salmon around for a while, daydreaming about what it would be like to be a real bear and snag a live salmon thrashing its way up a wild stream; maybe in another incarnation. The thought of food reminded me that the Three Dog Bakery was just a few blocks away.

When I arrived, the 3-D was packed—no pun intended. A chocolate Lab was drooling copiously all over the glass dessert case; a pair of Italian Greyhounds were sniffing the cookie counter, trying to decide what to have; and a friendly Dalmatian named Spot informed me that today's special was the German Shepherd's Pie. So I had some of that along with a side of Poodle Noodles and three Corgi Crumpets for dessert. The guys at the 3-D Bakery know me, and my credit is good: if only they'd let me have a doggie bag.

Normally, after gorging myself like that, I'd find a soft spot and curl up for a nice digestive nap. But the inspiring sight of the Space Needle caught my eye and, having sniffed someplace that Dogs from all over the world come to mark, I decided to make my own little pilgrimage. It being the height of tourist season, I had to spend a full half hour in order to sniff all the messages on the big spike. One was from an Australian Cattle Dog named Dundee who wanted to know where he could find a herd of cows to chase. Another was from Igor, a big Irish Wolfhound advertising his stud services (he smelled extremely intact). There was also a snotty note from a pretentious French Poodle who had nothing but negative comments about the local cuisine. *Mon Chien!*

Gazing up at the Space Needle made me wonder what my hometown looked like from way up there. As if on cue, the elevator doors opened and, without thinking, I hopped inside and hid in the back of the car for the long ride up. At the top, the elevator doors opened onto an enormous restaurant full of smells so delicious I nearly drooled all over myself.

I approached one of the big booths and asked the well-padded couple seated there for a sample of their juicy prime rib. Big mistake! You might have thought I was a werewolf baring fangs and foaming at the mouth the way they reacted to my polite little beg. The woman inhaled her martini olive (nearly choking on it), and the man yelled, "Waiter! There is a DOG at our table!" loud enough for the entire restaurant to hear, which, of course, brought the entire wait staff rushing over.

I excused myself by scooting under the table and pressing up against the back of the booth. Six waiters dropped to their hands and knees and peered at me under the white linen tablecloth. They looked as confused as I felt, but all of a sudden one of the waiters made a grab for me and I realized that my only escape route was overland. I jumped onto the booth between the stingy couple (unable to resist snatching a juicy slab of the woman's prime rib while I was at it) then bounded across the adjoining table, where the "take-out" I was dragging toppled wine and water goblets and—alas—I had to let it go to keep on running.

The place erupted in pandemonium as I bolted for the elevator. More waiters yelled, "Get the dog! Get the dog!!" while crashing into each other and flinging crab cocktails and lamb chops to the floor (oh, how I would have loved to sample those). Even the kitchen staff came out and tried to catch me! It was only by the width of a whisker that I managed to squeeze between the closing elevator doors. It was one of those rare times that I was grateful for not having more than an inch of tail.

No one in the elevator appeared to notice me and, not wanting to draw attention to myself, I huddled in a corner and tried to control my panting. The car was nearly back down to earth when a big oaf of a man wearing cowboy boots bigger than me managed to step on my paw. My yelp of pain gave me away, and the cowboy picked me up in a way that indicated he was clearly not a dog-person. "Hey," he drawled, "What kinda varmit is this?" "Rats!" I thought, silently pleading to Saint Bernard for a timely distraction. There I was, hanging in mid air with everyone looking at me quizzically, when a dog-friendly-looking lady said, "Why, it's a Schipperke! And isn't she just the cutest thing! Here, let me have her."

As she reached for me the elevator made a terribly bumpy landing, and I was (to use football jargon) fumbled. Landing on all fours, I made an end run past the clumsy cowboy and dashed out as the doors opened, sprinting for the park exit.

That call was way too close: definitely time for a little less human interaction. My nose picked up the salty scent of the Pacific, and I decided that a walk on the beach and maybe a run at a few shore birds was in order. With legs on cruise control, I headed west.

En route to the beach I came across a sign that read Hiram M. Chittenden Locks. "Great," I thought, "I could use a snack," and went in. Well, I swear, all I could see was an enormous rectangular pool full of boats: no bagels, no cream cheese, and no lox. I did, however, pick up the unmistakable stink of Norwegian rats hiding out on a dismal looking Dutch barge in the water below. What luck! My dream of chasing the pointy-nosed little vermin off a barge to drown in the sea was about to be realized.

I ran back and forth, barking, "You dirty rat! You dirty rat!" (I do a pretty good James Cagney impersonation and I had the rats quivering real good, see?) Only problem was, the barge was too far below. Then, as if Dog in heaven knew my frustration, water started flooding into the pool and the barge slowly began to float up!

I was so excited, the fur on my hackles stood straight up—Mohawk style. The rats were good and panicked now, squealing and tripping all over themselves looking for a place to hide. The barge continued floating steadily up and was almost within range. "Any second now," I told myself, getting ready to make my Super Schipperke soaring leap. "Steady ... easy ... watch it. Okay, ready ... set ... Hey! What the ...?" Suddenly the barge was moving quickly away from the side— out of range.

"Come back here you dirty little rats!" I barked ferociously. But seeing that they were safe, they stood up on their scrawny hind legs and thumbed their pointed little noses at me as they sailed away. "NO, NO, NO!" I whined. It was all too humiliating. This Chittenden place, besides having no bagels, cream cheese, or smoked salmon, was no fun at all.

Trying not to dwell on my defeat, I resumed my journey to the shore. Halfway there, I felt my throat getting dry—must have been all that barking. I detoured into a park looking for water, but found something far better: a family picnic, complete with hotdogs and a water bowl belonging to a gorgeous German Shepherd, named Rolph. He had Rin Tin Tin eyes. As I lapped from Rolph's bowl he made seductive little bow plays and begged shamelessly for me to play with him. After a few rounds of free-style wrestling the humans tossed us each half a hotdog (needed catsup) then I heard the humans say, "Do you think it's lost? Maybe we should call the SPCA." Rolph or no Rolph, it was time to cut this visit short. I gave the big German a farewell lick and dashed down the road towards the sea.

Feeling re-energized by Rolph, the hotdog, and the smell of the salty air, I sprinted all the way to the beach. What a beach it was, too! Wide and windy, and full of birds standing around just waiting to be chased. First, I stood at the surf line, nose in the air, looking majestic, and sniffed all the exotic smells wafting in from far across the Pacific. Next, I drove shore birds back and forth at the edge of the waves as they tried to poke their beaks into the sand. Curious about what they found so interesting down there, I dug a few exploratory pits of my own, then watched, fascinated, as they filled up with water.

I was so mesmerized by the water-sand inter-play that I never noticed the rogue wave that sneaked up behind me. If there is a moral to this story, it is this: Never turn your tail to the sea. One second, I was paw-deep in water; the next, I was tumbling head over tail, blinded by frothy murk, thrashing wildly, my lungs burning for air, not knowing which way was up. As my pitifully short life flashed before my eyes I realized that I wasn't ready to die: there were so many more lamp posts to smell, so many more big dogs to meet, so many more rats to be dispatched. So I begged Saint Bernard to save my soggy hide just one more time, promising in exchange to be a really, really "Good Dog" from here on out. As I began to inhale what I was sure would be a lung-ful of brine, I popped to the surface like a furry cork and felt sweet air rush in instead.

Gasping for breath and thrashing in the turbulence, I thought, not surprisingly, of rats being chased off a barge. I shook water from my eyes and swam frantically in circles, trying to find the shore. When I finally located it,

from atop a long rolling wave, it looked very, very far away. And, between it and me were more killer waves. I wasn't sure I could swim back through them. But what choice did I have? "Steady on, SheBear," I told myself. "You've been in worse situations, haven't you?" Well, no, actually I hadn't, but this was no time to worry about silly details.

I paddled shoreward with dogged determination (again, no pun intended), using every ounce of muscle and will power I possessed for what seemed like a dog's year. Unfortunately, every time a rolling wave lifted me up so I could see the shore again, it looked further away. Was I caught in a rip tide? What was a rip tide, anyway? Or was this the Twilight Zone, the Bermuda Triangle?!

"Pull yourself together, SheBear," I told myself. "You can do this, just don't panic." That's when I felt it: a little bump of panic. Something grazed along my side. It had an investigatory sense to it, like the first sniff from an unfamiliar dog. Or like the bump a shark might make when determining if you'd be good to eat. Shark? Shark?! Did somebody say shark!? "Nooooo!" I howled, imagining a gaping jaw full of crooked, razor-sharp teeth chomping down on me like I was a crouton. I thought I was going to wee in the water. Instead, a sudden burst of energy coursed through me, propelling me through the water like Mark Spitz-Hound. I mean to say, I was moving! Practically flying over the water!

My joy dissolved when I looked down and saw air between the water and me, and I realized that I truly was flying over the water. I must be in the shark's jaws and he must be parading me around on the surface for all his sharky friends to see (like a 15-pound Schipperke was some big catch!). I flashed on those hapless humans in the movie, "Jaws," then thought that this shark had a very soft mouth (maybe he was a Retriever Shark?) because I felt no pain. A sensation of being held, but no teeth sinking into me, no shark breath gagging me. Still, I yelped and snarled and wriggled. Hell if I was gonna go down that fat fish's gullet without a decent dog fight!

I was about to sink my incisors into what was likely to be my last bite, when I heard a voice say, "Hey, take it easy little guy, it's okay! I'm not going to hurt you." "Wait a minute," I thought. "Sharks don't talk! Well, except for those land sharks on Saturday Night Live re-runs. But how did a land shark get out here in the middle of the Pacific?" I was still struggling when I heard Mr. Shark say, "Okay, I got you now, fella. What are you doing way out here?"

The next thing I saw was a man's face. A man! Not a shark? No, not a shark! A man. A man in a kayak! A man in a kayak who had just fended off the savage land shark and saved me from a horrible death! The man set me down in his kayak and told me not to rock the boat. I was so happy to be alive I climbed all over the guy, licking his face lavishly, and whining gratefully. He accepted my licks good-naturedly, but when I shook myself to dry off he muttered, "Aaah, *!#@, thanks a lot!" Panting happily, I put my paws up on the edge of the cockpit, and for the next half an hour the man paddled us towards a marina while I watched birds and barked at boats.

We glided smoothly into a slip alongside a sleek sailboat and the man yelled, "Hey there, BraveHeart! How ya doin' boy? Look what I found!" Then I saw HIM: the most handsome Husky in the Pacific Northwest, trotting towards me, his long tail swooshing, and—swoon—his name was BraveHeart. And, darn it! I was having a very bad fur day.

The man set me up on the dock and I tried vainly to shake my fur into some semblance of style before BraveHeart could get a closer look. The big Bow-Wow lumbered over and gave me a very friendly sniff. I was about to return the compliment when the man swooped me up in a thick towel and carried me onboard the sailboat, BraveHeart close behind. The man sat me in his lap and carefully dried me off as BraveHeart and I gazed into each other's eyes. After reading my nametag and putting me down on the floor, the man said, "BraveHeart, meet the amazing ocean-swimming SheBear!" I rolled right onto my back and growled softly, in my most seductive Mae West Highland White imitation, "Hello, Big Boy." To which BraveHeart wagged his enormous tail and panted heavily.

He and I were just getting better acquainted when I heard the man say, "Hello? Is this Elise? Hi, Elise, my name is Brian. I found your dog, SheBear."

My heart leapt: Elise! The man was on the phone talking to my Elise! As captivating as BraveHeart was, I tore myself away and jumped up on Brian's lap, barking excitedly into the phone.

"Hey! Elise!" I yipped. "It's me, SheBear, and I had the best day ever! I ate breakfast at the café, met the Interurban dog, chased the Really Big Cats at the zoo, and ran agility at the park. Pant, pant, pant! Then I swam in the lake, played Frisbee with the frat guys, and hunted squirrels in the park with a friendly Cocker…"

I was leaping all over Brian's lap while he tried to shield the phone so he could keep talking to Elise, but that didn't stop me from telling her all about my adventure.

"…oh, yeah, and I almost had tea in a B&B, and I did eat ice cream from a truck, and I met a really weird girl on Broadway…pant, pant…and there was a dog catcher in Pioneer Square, so I went to Pike Place for salmon and then over to the 3-D Bakery for lunch. Woof! Did I sniff some amazing news at the Space Needle! I even went up to the top for a bit of prime rib. Pant, pant, pant. Then I chased rats off a barge, and ate hotdogs with Rolf… pant, pant. And, and, oh yeah, I went body surfing, too. That's where I met Brian!"

Brian stood up (leaving me on the comfy berth) laughing, and said, "Yeah, she's fine, just a little excited, I think." He patted my head as Elise fired off more questions, but I could only hear his end of the conversation.

"Well, it was the strangest thing," he said. "I was kayaking off the beach and there she was, out past the breakers, swimming towards shore…."

Meanwhile, I continued with my monologue to Elise: "…and Brian took me back to his boat to meet BraveHeart. Pant, pant, pant. Elise, you should meet BraveHeart, he is soooo gorgeous, I think I'm in love!"

Brian was saying into the receiver, "I have know idea out how she got out there, but she was pretty frantic so I picked her up and brought her back to my boat….Sure, come on over and get her now. She and BraveHeart— that's my dog—are getting along great, but I bet she'd love to see a familiar face."

Brian gave Elise directions to his boat and hung up the phone as I was saying to Elise, "Come HERE, Elise! Brian smells really nice, and he's got this really great boat; it's a sailboat, Elise —that means it can go places, not like our houseboat that doesn't go anywhere—and…"

"Hey, hey, it's okay, SheBear! Elise is coming," he told me, gently stroking my drying fur. I yipped at him happily, then jumped down to tell BraveHeart more details about my day's adventures.

While waiting for Elise to arrive, Brian fed BraveHeart and me each a bowl of (wouldn't you know it!) vegetarian dog food. Then, exhausted, I fell happily asleep in BraveHeart's big soft doggie bed.

I was awakened from a lovely dream (BraveHeart and I were romping together off-leash) by the excited voice of Elise. "SheBear!" she yelled, picking me up, hugging and kissing me hard; she sometimes forgets that I weigh only 15 pounds. Then she put on her stern, parental face and said, in a tone that was supposed to sound scolding, "You bad girl! How did you get out there in the ocean? How did you even get off of the porch?"

I just licked her face appeasingly.

When she was finished admonishing me she turned to Brian and hugged him as enthusiastically as only Elise can hug someone. She chanted, "Thank you-thank-you-thank-you-thank-you-THANK-YOU!" My mistress can be so embarrassing when she gets all wound up. Brian looked rather pleased, though, and he gave Elise a look that made her face turn all flushed—the way it does when she meets someone who smells really good to her.

Over dinner, Brian and Elise laughed and talked about me and BraveHeart, kayaks and houseboats, travel and food. When there was no more chow to beg for, BraveHeart and I climbed up to the cool of the deck to watch the moon rise. I was so exhausted from my adventures that all I could do was curl up next to the big Husky and fall fast asleep.

I began having the strangest dream: some rats were being chased by a dog catcher, who was being chased by a Big Cat, who was being chased by two Weimaraners in a Humvee, who were being chased by a land shark, who was being chased by me, when Elise woke me up. She said I had to say good night to BraveHeart and Brian. "Why?" I whined in protest. BraveHeart whined, too. I will never figure out why humans who obviously like the smell of each other have to say good night.

Riding home in the car, Elise looked at me and said, "SheBear, you little sneak! I'm fixing that gate first thing in the morning! Well, maybe first thing in the afternoon. Okay, first thing whenever I get up. Anyway, no more leash-less outings for you! You had me worried to death. I hope you realize that if it hadn't been for Brian you might have drowned out there. God, I'm glad you're all right!" She patted me lovingly, and I licked her face.

Then she said, "You like BraveHeart, don't you? You little flirt!"

"Flirt?" I barked. "Look who's talking!"

"Brian is pretty cute, isn't he?" she asked.

I did a little shiver, then sighed.

After another minute, she turned to me and said, "Look, if you ever decide to take off on another adventure—take me with you, okay?"

I sat up and barked excitedly, "Actually, I'm meeting BraveHeart at the dog park at sunrise tomorrow; want to come?"

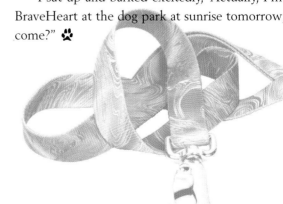

LAB
COATS

What the most popular breed in America is wearing.

Available at EDDIE BOWWOW

all THE PRESIDENTS' DOGS

(well, some of them, anyway)

"The country at large takes a natural interest in the President's dogs and judges him by the taste and discrimination he shows in his selection.... Any man who does not like dogs and want them about does not deserve to be in the White House." —American Kennel Club Gazette, 1924

BY
ROVER
WASHINGTON

It has been said that the Presidency is the loneliest job in the world. And what human would want to tackle that kind of work without a trusted canine confidante? The smarter ones didn't. Of the 43 U.S. Presidents, 33 kept dogs in the White House. Among the five or so Presidents that were not dog fanciers was Harry S. Truman. Ironically, it was Harry who said, "If you want a friend in Washington, get a dog." Rather than take his own advice, though, he rejected the gift of a Cocker spaniel puppy named FELLER, given to him by a Missouri woman who apparently thought he really did need a friend in the White House.

"If you want a friend in Washington, get a dog."
—*Harry S. Truman*

$\mathcal{L}$et Canine Academy help you earn a PhD (Phido Degree) and find a rewarding career in one of these exciting fields:

- Paper Shredder
- Lap Dog
- Excavator
- Dog Food Taste Tester
- Bed Warmer
- Show Dog
- Personal Trainer
- Date Bait
- Nanny Dog
- Pet Therapist
- Mascot
- Stud

Canine Academy

First Dogs have helped their Presidents to win office, save uncertain political careers, shape national and international policy, impress visiting dignitaries, and even escape tedious Oval Office meetings. Just as importantly they have helped preserve their masters' sanity by reminding them how to laugh, sing, and act un-presidentially goofy. This article is dedicated to all the many First Dogs who have had a paw in keeping our nation sane and sovereign. Unable to list them all, the following is merely a brief description of some of the more famous (or infamous) Presidential Pups.

> *"I care not for a man's religion whose dog and cat are not the better for it."*
> —*Abraham Lincoln*

FIDO LINCOLN was Abraham Lincoln's yellow-brown mongrel, and the first Presidential dog to have his photo taken. Because the country dog didn't take well to the noisy city of Washington, Lincoln sent him back to Springfield, Illinois (where he was well cared for by friends) and Abe and his two sons had to be satisfied with Fido's photo. The President once said, "I care not for a man's religion whose dog and cat are the better for it."

GRIM HAYES was a Greyhound, one of the many dogs who lived in the Rutherford B. Hayes White House. Whoever named the dog was, perhaps, prescient: the hound was hit by a train and killed instantly. Dog lovers from around the country responded to the President's loss by flooding the White House with condolences.

DASH HARRISON, a Collie, made himself comfortable in a very fancy dog house installed next to the White House by President Benjamin Harrison.

SKIP ROOSEVELT, a mongrel (perhaps a Rat terrier), was discovered by Teddy Roosevelt during a bear-hunting trip in the Grand Canyon. He was a favorite of the President's numerous dogs, which ranged in size from ROLLO, a Saint Bernard, to

President Harding's Airedale, *Laddie Boy*, seated on a high-backed chair on the White House Lawn, ca. 1921-23.
Photo courtesy of the Ohio Historical Society

MANCHU, a Pekingese given to Teddy's daughter by the Empress Dowager Ci-Xi of China. There was also PETE, a Bull terrier who almost ripped the pants off of the French Ambassador. And SAILOR BOY, a Chesapeake Bay retriever, who would swim after the presidential yacht if it sailed without him.

LADDIE BOY HARDING was Warren Harding's beloved Airedale and a very political pet. He greeted diplomats on the White House steps and sat in on Cabinet meetings in his own hand-carved ladder-backed chair. Laddie may have been the first First Dog to enjoy a birthday party attended by other Washingtonian dogs, and celebrated with a layer cake made of dog biscuits. The First Lady, Florence, would roll up the morning paper, give it to Laddie, and tell him, "Take this to Warren." For exercise, the Airedale retrieved golf balls that the President hit on the White House lawn.

PRUDENCE PRIM and ROB ROY COOLIDGE were two white Collies belonging to President Coolidge and First Lady, Grace. Avid dog lovers, the Coolidges had 12 dogs during their White House years, some of whom made sport of chasing maids throughout the halls of the residence. Prudence, elegantly attired in bonnet and bow, would accompany the First Lady during the annual White House Easter egg-rolling contests. Rob Roy (bribed with treats from Grace) posed with her for her official portrait painted by the famous artist, Howard Chandler Christy.

KING TUT HOOVER, Herbert Hoover's police dog, helped win the presidency for his master by posing with him in a highly successful campaign photo that was circulated by the thousands. Hoover wasn't just using the handsome Tut as a photo prop though: he truly loved dogs and had at least nine during his presidency.

FDR and his little dog *Fala* go for a drive in Hyde Park, NY, 1944.
Photo: Corbis

...Johnson once said, "You know there is no one in the world I would rather sleep with than Yuki."

FALA ROOSEVELT was perhaps the most famous White House dog, and Franklin Delano Roosevelt's ever-present companion. The popular Scotty shook paws with visiting dignitaries, stood at attention when the Star Spangled Banner played, received his own fan mail, and even witnessed the signing of the Atlantic Charter. He slept next to the President's bed, and is portrayed sitting beside his master at the FDR Memorial in Washington, D.C.

WINKS ROOSEVELT was another of FDR's many dogs (he had at least nine). A Llewellin setter with a big appetite, Winks managed to wolf down 18 bacon and egg breakfasts "quick as a wink" before being caught by the White House staff.

HEIDI EISENHOWER was a Weimeraner who suffered from a weak bladder. After a few disrespectful accidents on President Dwight D. Eisenhower's diplomatic carpet, she was sent back to the farm in Gettysburg, Pennsylvania, leaving **SPUNKY THE SCOTTIE** in charge. Perhaps it was little Spunky who inspired the famous Eisenhower quote, "What counts is not necessarily the size of the dog in the fight but the size of the fight in the dog."

CHARLIE KENNEDY, a Welsh terrier, was John Fitzgerald Kennedy's favorite dog and an important aide. "I was there in Jack Kennedy's office that day. Everything was in an uproar. I was ten feet from Kennedy's desk as Pierre Salinger [the press secretary] ran around the office taking messages and issuing orders while the President sat looking awfully worried. There was talk about the Russian fleet coming in and our fleet blocking them off. It looked like war. Out of the blue, Kennedy suddenly called for Charlie to be brought to his office." (Traphes Bryant, White House kennel-keeper describing Oval Office events during the Cuban missile crisis.) Later on, Charlie fell in love with **PUSHKINKA**, a Russian mongrel given to JFK's young daughter, Caroline, by Nikita Khrushchev in an effort to help ease tensions between the two nations. Together, the First Dogs produced four "**PUPNIKS**," as President Kennedy called them. The Kennedys had one of the largest packs of dogs in the White House since Teddy Roosevelt's reign.

HIM & HER JOHNSON was a pair of Beagles belonging to President Lyndon Johnson. He no doubt adored the hounds, but when he picked them up by

"What counts is not necessarily the size of the dog in the fight but the size of the fight in the dog."
—Dwight D. Eisenhower

Comfortable • Life-like • Studly

buddy balls

1-800-BBALLS
(discreet brown package delivery)

they're the Perfect *Fix*

President Ford and his dog, *Liberty*, in the Oval Office, 1974.

Photo courtesy of the Gerald R. Ford Library

various improper campaign gifts, including the dog: "A man down in Texas heard Pat on the radio mention the fact that our two daughters would like to have a dog. And believe it or not, the day before we left on this campaign trip we got a message from Union Station in Baltimore saying they had a package for us. We went down to get it. You know what it was? It was a little cocker spaniel in a crate that he sent all the way from Texas, … and our little girl, Tricia, the six-year-old, named it Checkers. And you know the kids love the dog and I just want to say this, right now, that regardless of what they [the Press] have to say about it, we are going to keep it."

KING TIMAHOE NIXON, an Irish setter, was another of Nixon's dogs. The King was temporarily demoted to mere "Timahoe," but only for the duration of Prince Charles' White House visit. In a memo to his staff, Nixon wrote, "During the Prince's visit, King Timahoe will be referred to only as Timahoe, since it would be inappropriate for the Prince to be outranked by a dog."

LIBERTY FORD (a highly appropriate name for a First Dog) was a close friend and confidante to President Gerald Ford. The Golden retriever (Ford's favorite breed) was brought in whenever the President needed to "conclude" a tediously long Oval Office meeting. Like her master, Liberty was athletic and took full advantage of the various White House swimming facilities (including the indoor pool and the more refreshing outdoor fountain).

GRITS CARTER was a mixed-breed dog given to President Carter's young daughter, Amy, by one of her school teachers. Unfortunately, Grits was not cut out for presidential duty. He made a terrible scene during a White House-publicized Heartworm Awareness Week campaign by tearing off his muzzle and refusing to let the vet get near him. Who can blame the guy? Grits wasn't exactly White House-broken either, so he was eventually returned to the teacher.

their long ears he incurred the outrage of thousands of American dog lovers who insisted it was cruel treatment. Beagles were a popular breed with Johnson; there was **LBJ** (Little Beagle Johnson), FRECKLES (son of Him), and EDGAR, given to LBJ by FBI Director, J. Edgar Hoover.

"Liberty quickly became an Oval Office fixture, often reclining right next to the President's desk when she wasn't taking care of visitors who had overstayed their welcome."

—Roy Rowan & Brooke Janis

YUKI JOHNSON was perhaps LBJ's favorite dog. The mutt was found wandering around a Texas gas station by LBJ's daughter, Luci, who rescued him and brought him to Washington. Yuki quickly enchanted the President with his "Texas accent." The two would sing duets together to the amusement of Oval Office visitors. About the dog, Johnson once said, "You know there is no one in the world I would rather sleep with than Yuki."

CHECKERS NIXON, a black and white Cocker spaniel, may not have been a true First Dog, but he deserves mention here because he helped save Nixon's vice-presidency, enabling him to go on to become the 37th President. In the famous televised Checkers Speech, Nixon defended himself from accusations that he received

REX REAGAN. King of the dogs? Well, king of the regal Reagan clan at least during their Royal White House reign. Rex happened to be a pure-bred King Charles spaniel, a diminutive little dog that fitted the petite stature of Queen Nancy far better than their previous canine—a large and rambunctious Sheepdog named Lucky who ended up (luckily for him) residing at the Reagans' Santa Barbara ranch where he could roam and be as rowdy as he wanted to be. Back in the White House, little Rex was treated like a king; pampered by day and retiring at night to his private dog house, which had been specially designed for him by the fabulous interior designer, Theo Hayes (a relative of the dog-loving President, Rutherford B.).

MILLIE BUSH. If there's anydoggy out there who does not know who Millie is, raise your paw. Every dog should know about Millie. This spunky brown and white Springer spaniel was a great friend to President George Bush and the First Lady, Barbara. She met with celebrities from around the globe, chased White House squirrels, and appeared on the cover of Life Magazine along with her six puppies. Despite the stigma of being voted by Washingtonian Magazine as the "ugliest dog in Washington," she went on to write a national best-seller, "Millie's Book," which even outsold the Prez's own memoirs.

BUDDY CLINTON arrived in the White House just weeks before the Lewinsky scandal broke. Too bad the chocolate lab didn't get there earlier; he certainly would have been a more appropriate little friend for President Bill to play with. The fact that "he spent more time under the President's desk than any intern" might have prevented Bill from engaging in all those sexcapades. Buddy may not have had the literary talents of Millie, but he was featured in a fabulously popular book titled, "Dear Socks, Dear Buddy: Kids' Letters to the First Pets." Sadly, after his White House tenure, Buddy met an all too common doggie fate: he was hit by a car while playing car chase in his New York neighborhood.

The year is 2003 and BARNEY and SPOT BUSH are the current canine White House residents. Barney, a young Scotty, enjoys helping the Secret Service boys with security issues almost as much as he enjoys playing ball on the White House lawn with "W." Spot, a Springer spaniel (one of Millie's offspring), was actually born in the White House in 1989, and no doubt she feels right at home enjoying free run of the House. Both dogs are important members of the Bush First (or is it the Second Bush?) Family. 🐾

The Reagans being greeted by their dog, *Rex*, after arriving in the helicopter (Marine-1), 1986.
Photo courtesy of the Ronald Reagan Library

President Bush walks on the South Lawn of the White House, followed by *Millie* and her puppies, 1989.
Photo courtesy of the George Bush Presidential Library

Millie Bush was voted the "ugliest dog in Washington" by Washington Magazine *...but went on to write a best-seller, "Millie's Book"*

boxing LESSONS

1

2

by *Champion Boxing Bitch*
BONITA LA RUED

1 Find a willing sparring partner. Chase him down if you have to! I found this handsome mutt in the City Park.

2 Explain proper boxing etiquette, partiularly the "no teeth" rule. Some dogs, like this bad boy, must be taught how to fight fair.

3 Deliver a quick one-two punch to get the upper paw.

4 Distract your opponent any way you can. Use your wily charms, if you have any. Remember, anything goes in a dog fight.

5 Assume the dominant position and **declare yourself Top Dog!**

3

4

5

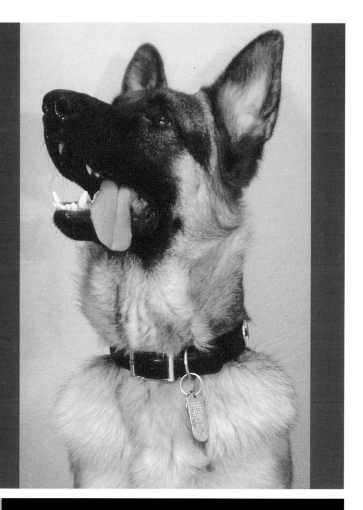

Quit begging.

Get the card.

Master's Card

HELP YOURSELF BOOKS

The largest selection of canine self-help titles in the world.

Located on the corner of Borders and Barns.

Come on in and bowse!

Conversations with Dog

Don't Sniff the Small Stuff
And it's All Small Stuff

Zen in the Art of Marking

THE COMPLETE IDIOT'S
GUIDE TO DOOR KNOBS

Survival of the Fluffiest

Dogma for Dummies

Stink and Grow Rich!

Life's Little Destruction Book

Understanding The Master's Mind

Why Table Legs Turn Us On

By
HUMPHREY
WOODS

Y

ou are passionately engaged with the dining room table leg, oblivious to the world around you and lost in lust when you hear the voice of your mistress screaming, "Humphrey, you pervert! Stop that this instant!" You try to disengage, you really do, but the urge to mate with the leg is so powerful that you continue humping ecstatically until yanked off by the scruff of your neck, tossed in the corner, and given one of those shake of the finger gestures (who knows what they mean?) Sound familiar?

The experience I just described is called **Table-leg Turn-on Syndrome**, or **TTS**, a surprisingly common affliction that causes dogs to become highly aroused by common everyday table legs. Well, are you a pervert? Technically, maybe. It depends on your definition of the word. More importantly, it depends on whether you care about the definition of the word. If you do not, then you are not a pervert. If you do, then you are not a dog.

Although TTS can affect any dog, no matter their breed, age or gender, it is most common among "fixed" (a misnomer if there ever was one!) dogs who are, understandably, sexually frustrated. These dogs have had very few, if any, sexual experiences and, not surprisingly, suffer from feelings of insecurity, inadequacy and the bitter knowledge that all their carefully cultivated bad habits will not be passed on to future generations of puppies.

Research has shown that there are **five basic reasons** why table legs turn us on:

First, they are tall, presenting a physical challenge that can only be dealt with by mounting them.

Second, they cannot run away.

Third, they cannot resist your advances by growling, snarling or biting.

Fourth, they come in a wide variety of sizes, shapes, styles, and some are erotically padded.

Fifth, they are often scent-marked by other dogs or drooling toddlers.

A TTS attack can strike without warning, quickly diminishing you to a pathetic humping machine. Overwhelmed with lust, you will try to have your way with the leg, completely unaware of how stupid you look doing it. How long an attack lasts depends on your energy level, the behavior of the table leg, and distractions, such as the sound of a can opener, or being rudely yanked away by your mistress. The severity of the disease can be determined by your reaction once an attack is over. In the early stages you will feel satisfied, but mildly disoriented, basically looking like an idiot until some distraction (such as the sound of a can opener) snaps you out of it. With moderate TTS the sense of satisfaction will be replaced somewhat by feelings of shame and you may begin to question your sexual orientation. In full-blown TTS you will continue to leer at the leg, panting heavily and waiting anxiously for your human to leave the room so that you can resume humping.

TTS is a progressive disease and should not go untreated. If you suspect that you suffer from TTS, join a local Table-Legs Anonymous pack. TA has an excellent 12-step program to help you conquer your disorder. If you think you require more help, consider the services of a professional Licensed Humping Therapist experienced in TTS disorder. If the problem still persists, you will probably have to eliminate all contact with table legs by moving permanently into the dog house. 🐾

Humphrey Woods is a licensed, clinical Humping Therapist who has helped hundreds of Dogs surmount their debilitating table-leg issues.

Chase the Pamplona Bulls as they run wild in the streets of Spain. Don't miss out on the fun!

Get your Master to call 1-800-GOBULL for reservations

reggie's excavation service

Why not let Reggie do your dirty work for you?

giving
puss the boot

BY DR. BAILY MACGROWELL

"The trouble with a kitten is that
eventually it becomes a cat."
~ Ogden Nash

You fetch them their slippers (okay, maybe a little drooled and chewed on, but you do fetch them). You enthusiastically help dig up the garden without even being asked. And you eagerly dispose of those leftovers that no one else wants to eat. In short, you are the best companion a human could ever want. Then one day, for absolutely no good reason, your human brings home a kitty. One of those self-centered and totally unnecessary creatures who will make it her mission to destroy your domestic bliss. Do you have to sit, roll over, or play dead when this happens? We say NO! (Well, actually we say "Aaarrrfff!" but we mean NO!) We say,

"Don't just sit there with your tongue hanging out—take action!"

1. The Cat's Out of the Bag

When your human brings the new kitty home for the first time, let him know it is a BIG mistake. There are two basic approaches, depending on your breed. Terriers and other high-energy types should employ the insanity strategy. You know, tear around the room at full speed while yapping excitedly, showing a lot of fang. More sedate breeds should use the, "Oh, why hast thou forsaken me?" approach: Whimper mournfully, hang your head and give your human your best dejected look. Important: No matter how interesting the kitty smells, DO NOT go around sniffing it or wagging your tail. (No! Bad dog! No sniffing!) If you just can't stop yourself from sniffing, content yourself with a quick snuffle then give a disgusted snort and leave the room. If you fail to make your human get rid of the kitty, you'll have to move on to Step 2.

2. Scratch and Sniff

As you probably have learned, cats are compulsive scratchers—a habit that can be used to your advantage. Spy on the bewhiskered nuisance, and when you discover her shredding something particularly expensive (say, the new, imported silk draperies), run to your human, bark excitedly (but not so loudly that you alert the kitty), and tug at his clothing. Humans can be infuriatingly slow to pick up on the, "For God's sake, you idiot, Timmy has fallen down the well again, follow me!" signal, so be persistent. As your human surveys the damage, studiously sniff the shredded remains, then give a "Woooof!" and a "How much do you think THIS will cost to fix?" expression. HINT: If the kitty tries to flee the scene of the crime, block her escape route.

3. Cat-astrophe

If the kitten has been de-clawed or is a little goody-four paws that doesn't destroy stuff (this is highly unlikely) you will have to create your own cat-astrophe. Fetch kitty's play  mousy (make sure it's not your play mousy) and put it next to the antique crystal table lamp. Knock the lamp over with your tail (don't want to leave any telltale paw prints) and

begin barking excitedly. Once your human arrives on the scene to investigate, look pointedly from the kitty to her play mousy then give your human an indignant look. HINT: Do not, under any circumstances, start playing with the kitty's play mousy. If you do, and you get carried away and knock anything over, even one of those sappy Hummel figurines, you might end up in the dog house.

4. When Puss Comes to Shove

If, after all your efforts to discredit the kitty, your human decides to keep it anyway, you may as well make the best of it. Unless it's one of those snotty Siamese or Persian breeds, you might be able to have a little fun with your new house mate. Show kitty how to play "Slip-And-Slide" on the kitchen floor, or "You Bunny, Me Wolf." Slobber liberally on your kitty, she'll love this. See how high you can get her to jump out of a sound cat nap by barking at full volume right in her ear. HINT: If you knock anything over while you're playing, make sure the cat's play mousy makes its way to the scene of the crime. 🐾

Coming next: Can Curiosity Really Kill the Cat?

PEMBROKE'S SCHOOL OF HERDING
The Leaders of the Pack

Work with sheep, cattle, goats or small children. Beginning, intermediate and advanced courses.
Individualized instruction with videotaped feedback.

AT PSOH YOU WILL LEARN TO:

- ❋ Quicken your lunge
- ❋ Deepen your bark
- ❋ Give good eye

- ❋ Sharpen your nip
- ❋ Improve cornering skills
- ❋ Correct bad habits

CALL TODAY: 1-800-HERDEM

Feeling over the hill?

Sign up today and receive a Free copy of **Past Prime**, the newsletter that teaches **old dogs new tricks**.

Join the growing ranks of the AARF—**American Association of Retired Fidos**—because when you are old and gray, it pays to belong to a PAC with clout.

AARF

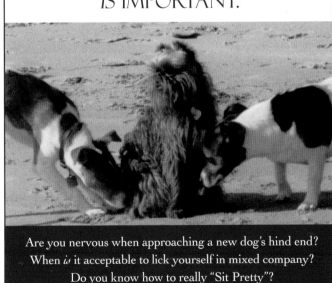

YOUR SNIFFING ETIQUETTE *IS* IMPORTANT.

Are you nervous when approaching a new dog's hind end?
When *is* it acceptable to lick yourself in mixed company?
Do you know how to really "Sit Pretty"?

CHAUNCY'S CHARM SCHOOL

If your manners leave something to be desired, call Chauncy

1.800.CHARMS

Peaky
wants to know…

"Do I look like the sort of dog who would let anyone pull anything over on me?"

"Oh Darling! Don't we look marvelous? We just love playing dress-up! Makes us feel so chic."

"You know, when your job is rounding up unruly pre-schoolers all day long, the right duds make all the difference."

"How do I feel? How do I feel? Well, as Fran Lebowitz so aptly put it, 'If you are a dog and your owner suggests that you wear a sweater …suggest that he wear a tail.'"

"Wooooff!
I look GOOOD!"

"I am a dog. I am very happy being a dog. I would be an even happier dog if my mistress did not feel compelled to dress me up in silly, unnatural outfits."

WANTED
BY THE FBI

 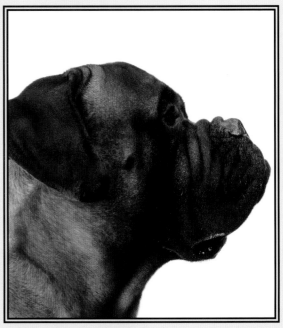

HECTOR

VIOLATIONS: Failure to appear when called, Obstruction of doorway, Reckless Drooling, Indecent Exposure in a public dog park, Resisting a bath, Possession of illegal Pugs, Grand Theft Lotto, Aiding and Abetting a known feline, Passing Gas in the slow lane, Walking without a license, Sexual Harassment of an inanimate object, Mailman fraud, Abduction of unattended beef Wellington, Solicitation

ALIASES: BadDogHector!, Drool Monger, Cannibal Hector
DOB: August 13, 2000
DESCRIPTION: Male Bullmastiff, 2'6" on all fours, 175 lbs., short fawn fur, brown eyes, black muzzle

OCCUPATION: Gigolo
REMARKS: Drools heavily and snores loudly
CAUTION: Hector can be extremely naughty and should be approached with caution or large dog biscuits.

IF YOU HAVE ANY INFORMATION CONCERNING THIS DOG PLEASE CONTACT YOUR LOCAL FBI OFFICE OR THE NEAREST ANIMAL SHELTER.

Doggerel

By Dogden Nash

I was walking with the big Airedale
A handsome beast with a chopped-off tail
When we came upon the Labradors
The ones that everyone adores

As we sniffed and wagged and said "Bow-wow"
From the bushes came a loud "Meow!"
A mighty ruckus did ensue
Involving a dog we know as Blue

Though old and short and quite rotund
Blue is a feisty little Dachshund
He lunged at the cat with outstretched paws
While trying to avoid her feline claws

Fur was flying, Yip, yip, yip!
The cat, it seemed, had a nasty nip
Old Blue let out horrific howls
From wounded, torn and bloody jowls

Then suddenly a harlequin cur
Sprang from nowhere with a great big "Gurrr"
He was a most statuesque Great Dane
Who seemed quite positively insane

Like a crazed, demented, obsessed fool
He pawed and barked and did he drool!
Unable to get close to the cat
The Dane stood by to do combat

Then along came big brash Johnnie Walker
The bold and All-American Cocker
Johnnie leapt into the fray
And, predictably, began to bray

His daring so excited Strudle
The charming Miniature Poodle
That she began to yap in fright
It really was an amazing sight

All the ruckus, all the sound
Woke the Catahoula Leopard hound
He'd been upon the hilltop sunning
But quick as a wink—Jake came running

Though normally not a hyper pup
Jake sensed that something big was up
Fearlessly he rushed the shrub
Thinking kitty might be tasty grub

It was difficult to see the fight
But what we heard gave us all a fright
We stood stock still with baited breath
Waiting for the smell of death

Jake did his best to get the cat
But as he emerged he said only, "Drat!
The feline fled, she got away
The sneaky, nimble nine-lived stray!"

Of course, this made the Pit Bull, Duke
Really, really, want to puke
"And," said Sam the mangy mutt,
"Why didn't you just grab her butt?"

Poor old Jake felt completely beat
Needing sympathy to ease defeat
It came from rolly-polly Yuppie
A wise, if somewhat youthful puppy

"My fellow doggies," Yup said, "Please!
Which one of us has not some fleas?
Which one of us could have done more?
Remember our esprit de corps!"

At that the pack did rally 'round
To sniff and lick the great old hound
Then Babbs, a bitch of doubtful breed,
Said she had some bones buried

We fell in line and followed her
Toward a hillside full of cockleburr
We dug happily for quite some time
Rewarded with a tasty mine

We must have looked a pack demented
Gnawing together so contented
When the sun went down, we said farewell
Agreeing that the day'd been swell

As the Airedale and I trotted
A cat ahead of us we spotted
I looked at him, "What do you think?"
He sighed and said, "I need a drink!"

I growled to make her run in fear
And laughingly we watched her rear
We let the pussy get away
For tomorrow is another day

Your CanineSign

BY GREAT DANE RUDHYAR

"He's got his head in the stars." How many times have you heard that said about our fellow dogs? Oh, wait, they don't say that. They say, "He's got his head in the toilet again!" But, wherever we may have our heads, the fact is that from Canis Major to Canis Minor, we dogs are linked to the stars. (Even a planet was named after one of us: Pluto!) And whether you believe in astrology or not, nothing turns a bitch on like asking her sign when you're sniffing her tail. So, to assist all of you mellow mutts in your conversational astrology, here are some insights into the canine constellations.

Aries the Airedale

March 21–April 19

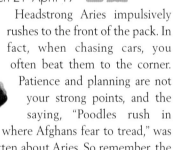

Headstrong Aries impulsively rushes to the front of the pack. In fact, when chasing cars, you often beat them to the corner. Patience and planning are not your strong points, and the saying, "Poodles rush in where Afghans fear to tread," was written about Aries. So remember, the next time you're chasing a moving van, ask yourself, "What will I do with this if I catch it?" Ruled by Mars, the god of war, you can be a hothead, so be careful when feeling hot under the collar that you don't bite the hand that feeds you. Your favorite color is gray and your favorite scent is fire.

Taurus the Bulldog

April 20–May 20

I don't want to say you're stubborn… but you are—unless you want to call it determined— which you can be if you're not being stubborn. Either way, once you dig in your paws, nothing short

of a bulldozer can move you. Do you ever lose at tug-of-war? Of course not. While not the most hair-raising beast on the block, you are earthy, practical and even poetic. You are also a steadfast friend, hence the phrase, "A dog's best friend is his Taurus" (or maybe his Mustang—so long as the window is rolled down). Your favorite color is gray and your favorite scent is bovine fertilizer.

Gemini the German Shepherd

May 21–June 21

If you could be in two places at once you would, and, in fact, sometimes it seems like you are. Gotta fetch Master's slippers…oh, look, there's a kibble left in my bowl…now where did I leave my squeaky toy?…hey, I need a walk! You are exuberant, always ready for fun, and a natural born wanderer. Being an air sign, you adore riding in the car sitting atop your Master's shoulder with your head out the window. If you're a Toy Poodle this is fine. If you are a Mastiff, it is not. Your favorite color is gray and your favorite scent is down wind.

Cancer the Collie

June 22–July 22

Your love of hearth and home is commendable, but for your own sake, and that of your Master, quit trying to rescue every Timmy that crosses your path! You

tend to be shy and moody, and at times you even play the martyr—refusing to come in from the cold just because Mistress complained about your shedding all over the sofa again. After all, you Cancer dogs pride yourselves on your good grooming. You are also very protective, generally cautious, and rather selective in your friends. Your favorite color is gray and your favorite scent is Beagles and lox.

Leo the Leonberger

July 23–August 22

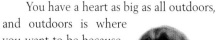

You have a heart as big as all outdoors, and outdoors is where you want to be because you hate feeling restricted. A natural ham actor, you are always performing. You have a flair that makes even your begging and rolling-over seem Shakespearean. And if your Master tells you to speak, you are likely to burst into a soliloquy from Hamlet. (Of course, as far as your Master is concerned, all you are saying is "Woof, woof! Ruff. Rrrrr…" but that's okay as long as you get the Milk-Bone.) Your favorite color is gray, your favorite smell is greasepaint and your favorite sound is the roar of the crowd.

Virgo the Vizsla

August 23–September 22

You can be described in three words: Or Gan Ized. Boy, are you organized! It drives you crazy when your toys get scattered all over the house, doesn't it? However, when it comes to romantic encounters you tend to be utterly impetuous. You are good with people, an excellent helper and a dependable companion, but you need to guard against feeling left out every time the fami-

ly goes off somewhere without you. Now, if you could only get over your hypochondria and quit sterilizing your water bowl, life would be so much more relaxed. Your favorite color is gray and your favorite scent is toilet water.

continued on page 78

Libra the Labrador
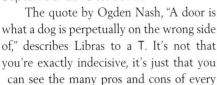
September 23–October 23

The quote by Ogden Nash, "A door is what a dog is perpetually on the wrong side of," describes Libras to a T. It's not that you're exactly indecisive, it's just that you can see the many pros and cons of every choice, and you need to weigh them on your Libra scales. Your sensual side has you forever seeking the ultimate ear scratch. You love beauty; however, your heavy-pawed attempts at interior decorating have not (as yet) been met with critical acclaim by your family. Your favorite color is gray and your favorite scent is cut grass.

Scorpio the Scottie
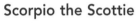
October 24–November 22

You are one intense little dog! Whether you are chasing rug rats around the yard or real rats around the barn, you do everything with 200% intensity. But your take-charge approach, coupled with that criminal little mind of yours, can land you in a pile of trouble, which, by the way, is not helped by your sometimes arrogant expression and pompous attitude. You come by your nature honestly though, ruled as you are by Pluto, that big, silly, goofy cartoon mutt...no wait, I mean, Pluto, the dark God of the underworld. Your favorite color is gray and your favorite scent is dirty rat.

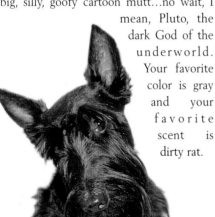

Sagittarius the Soft-coated Wheaten Terrier
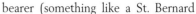
November 23–December 21

Despite the hair that sometimes obscures your eyes, you are a true visionary, and wise beyond your dog years—which is perhaps why you are so self-assured

and fearless when it comes to barking at unidentifiable noises. You are charming and quick-witted, but sometimes too blunt with your opinions. You love children and they are naturally attracted to you (mostly because they think you are a big stuffed animal until they get close enough to smell your breath). Your favorite color is gray and your favorite scent is dog breath.

Capricorn the Cocker Spaniel
December 22–January 19

You love to run. You especially love to run flocks of sheep, herds of goats and small companies of kindergartners. You are a natural Doggie CEO—the top dog, as it were. Ruled by Saturn, but tempered by Earth, your nature is a sound amalgamation of strength, sensitivity and order. Although you may be a bit of a plodder, you love a challenge, and are at your best under competitive pressure. Your sweet nature makes you

easy to get along with, yet you are reserved with strangers. Your favorite color is gray, and your favorite scent is the sweet smell of success.

Aquarius the Akita
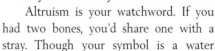
January 20–February 18

Altruism is your watchword. If you had two bones, you'd share one with a stray. Though your symbol is a water bearer (something like a St. Bernard with a keg attached to his collar), you are actually an air sign. That's one of the reasons you are always passing unnatural gas. You like new things and are very inventive; it was an Aquarian dog that invented the electric dog food can opener and the Frisbee made out of salami. (And although the Frisbalami never caught on, you have to admit it is a great idea!) Your favorite color is gray and your favorite scent is methane.

Pisces the Poodle
February 19–March 20

If you weren't a dog you'd be a fish. (Probably a dogfish chasing a catfish.) You love the water and would live in a dog houseboat if you could. You are also quite psychic, and when your Master is thinking about taking you for a walk you are already standing at the door with your

leash in your mouth. (Of course, when your Master is thinking about a nap, you are standing at the front door with your leash in your mouth. In fact, now that I think about it, you are always standing at the front door with your leash in your mouth. Hey, get a life!) You sometimes have difficulty distinguishing between dreams and reality, but, hey, as long as there's food in your dish and water in the toilet, why worry! Your favorite color is gray and your favorite scent is wet dog.

○ ◑ ● ◐ ○ While this information will not enable you to construct detailed astrology charts (largely because you cannot hold a pencil), it should give you enough information to get knee deep in doo-doo the next time you're chatting up an attractive Mexican Hairless at the Chi-Wa-Wa–Bar. Boning-up on your canine astrology will also help you to dazzle the pack at the full-moon howl-in' parties. 🐾

It was a sultry Saturday night and the Last Chance Rawhide Bar and Animal Shelter was packed. She cruised up on her Harley Sportster—wearing pure leather. Our eyes met. She said I had Rex-appeal. I hopped on the bike and never looked back.

AFGHAN LANDERS

NATURE ABHORS A VACUUM

Dear AFGHAN LANDERS,

Every week or so, my mistress lets that big, loud monster thing out of the hall closet and walks it all around the house. I don't understand why she even keeps the beast; it's dangerous. It growls and snarls and sucks up everything in its path—even staples and paper clips (which even I don't eat). It is absolutely maniacal! I've tried to warn her; I've barked and pulled on the thing's tail (which is disgustingly long and skinny and slimy), but she just gets all huffy and puts me outside. Mark my words, someday the fiend is going to turn on her, I just know it, I can sense these kinds of things. I think this brute has some sort of diabolical control over her. Can you recommend a good exorcist?
—Frightened, Frantic & Frenzied

Dear Frenzied,

You are a very brave Dog, but you should know better than to tangle with a Dirt Devil!

COP AN ATTITUDE

Dear AFGHAN LANDERS,

My human is a Finkerton security guard. He wants to be a cop. Late at night he takes me out driving in his "unmarked," as he calls it. He makes me sit in the back seat even though I get carsick. We end up in parts of town that Cujo wouldn't even roam. Then he drags me out of the car and we "patrol" seedy bars and dark junkyards while he barks commands at me in German—he thinks because I'm one quarter German shepherd I understand German (hey, I'm mostly Papillon). The big idiot is looking for trouble, and I want no part of it when he finds it. This Rambo thing is making me a nervous wreck. Help!
—Nervous Wreck

Dear Wreck,

If it makes you feel any better, you are not alone. Many humans have Rambo complexes. Unfortunately, some of them include their best friends in their fantasies. Here's what's going to happen: Your Rambo-man is eventually going to get into a nasty dog fight with some real Bad Guys, and when he does you'll need to stay out the fray. After that, he'll lick his wounds and stay home and watch reruns of Adam-12 and Dragnet. Just hang in there.

NO THANKS

Dear AFGHAN LANDERS,

What's a Golden retriever named Gold-Digger to do? All day long I wear my nails to the quick diggin' for buried treasure! And what kind of thanks do I get? They yell, "Digger, you *#%! dog, stop that digging this instant!!!"
—Unappreciated in the Back Yard

Dear Unappreciated,

If only our humans could smell what we smell and dig what we dig! Alas, their vision is weak and their nose is vestigial. Never mind, Gold-Digger, one day you will unearth the treasure buried deep in your yard, and on that day your master will eat his words.

Dear AFGHAN LANDERS,

Our next-door neighbors have the most tacky lawn statues imaginable. A badly proportioned, six-foot tall albino chipmunk stands in the middle of the front lawn welcoming visitors with outstretched arms and a buck-toothed grin. Behind him stands a gigantic lime green Tyrannosaurus Rex holding up a sickly tree fern. Swimming through the petunia bed is the dorsal fin of a great white shark (life size, of course). Naturally, I bark viciously every time we walk by this horrid menagerie—it's an eye sore. My master says, "Hush now, Alfred, they're not real." Good grief, how could anybody think they were real? My barks are in protest to the appalling bad taste of the statuary! I have a right to voice my opinion. How can I get Master to understand?
—Thoroughly Disgusted in New Jersey

Dear Disgusted,

Perhaps you should demonstrate your opinion in a more *marked* fashion?

Dear AFGHAN LANDERS,

Whenever I chase trespassing squirrels from my yard my mistress embarrasses me in front of all the neighbor dogs. She yells things like "Oh, good try, Rambler, you missed that one by only HALF a mile!" Then she laughs hysterically. She doesn't appreciate that at least I try, which is more than I can say for the cat. Anyway, can you recommend any pep pills, or other performance enhancers that will make me faster? Or, is there something I could put in the squirrel feeder to make them slower?
—Frustrated in Philadelphia

Dear Frustrated,

I do not condone drugs, not even for serious situations such as yours. However, I can recommend an excellent book called *Don't Chase The Small Stuff* by Teddy Bull Scratchmaster. His two-week program will improve your self-confidence by showing you how to go after more suitable prey, such as sloths and three-legged cows.

Dear AFGHAN LANDERS,

This is going to sound crazy, I know, but after a visit to the vet the other day, I woke up and noticed that both of my balls were missing (and I'm not talking about my

tennis balls). What would the vet want with a pair of Basset balls?
—*Ball-less in Baltimore*

Dear Ball-less,
Every year hundreds of Dogs report their balls missing after a hazily remembered visit to the vet, and there are almost as many theories explaining the bizarre disappearances. These theories range from the credible hypothesis that our balls end up in the Far East as some kind of aphrodisiac, to the laughable notion that removing our testicles somehow prevents us from having puppies. (Every Dog knows that only bitches can have puppies.) My personal opinion is that, disgusting as it sounds, the vets take our balls and play hacky sack with them on their lunch hour.

ALL DRESSED UP AND NO WHERE TO "GO"

Dear AFGHAN LANDERS,
Why do my people have to dress me up in stupid human outfits all the time? It makes it so hard to pee!
—*Over-dressed*

Dear Over-dressed,
Ever heard the term "clothes horse?" Kind of a misnomer— actually it's not a horse at all, but a human with a clothes fetish. These people will put clothing on everything— even their dogs! I bet your house is full of bed-skirts and dust jackets. Your people need to seek professional help! As for you, when nature calls, answer her by peeing right through those designer jeans.

Dear AFGHAN LANDERS,
I want to redecorate my dog house to impress the attractive little Papillon I'm dating. Do you know where I might find a stuffed Bengal tiger?
—*Hopeful Henry*

Dear Hopeful,
Papillons may be sexy little numbers, but they also happen to be highly intelligent. I doubt that she's going to fall for the old

"I chased it down on my African safari" story. Instead, why don't you hire a designer from Executive Dog Houses, Inc. to come in and help you out.

HOLY TURD?

Dear AFGHAN LANDERS,
I have been too embarrassed to ask anyone about this before, but my problem is really worrying me. My master and mistress collect my—as they call them—"tidings." They love me unconditionally, and they spoil me rotten, but collecting the droppings of an Old English sheepdog is going a bit far, don't you think? Could it be that they think my "tidings" are somehow valuable?
—*Flattered but Perplexed*

Dear Flattered,
Don't be so egotistical! Your humans collect your "tidings," and spread them around the perimeter of the yard as a booby trap for burglars.

Dear AFGHAN LANDERS,
I'm a healthy, young Welsh Corgi with absolutely nothing to herd. I've tried the children, the lawn statues, even the meter-reader, but none of these things are very satisfactory. Can you tell me where I can find a nice herd of cows?
—*Hurtin' to Herd*

Dear Hurtin',
Herds-R-Us has a wonderful, full-color catalog of herd-able livestock (and other unusual creatures) for every Dog's budget. Give them a call, and tell them I sent you.

Dear AFGHAN LANDERS,
Lately, on our walks, my mistress has begun to insist that I—a full-blooded Bloodhound—walk precisely at her side, not an inch ahead or behind. She never used to be so strict. This is torture! With a nose like mine I am hopelessly distracted by all the marvelous smells of the great outdoors. How can I get her to loosen up and let me "sniff the roses?"
—*Restrained & Straining*

Dear Restrained,
I am guessing that your mistress recently read a Dog obedience book of some sort. I am also guessing that you are big enough to keep up the pressure on your end of

Birthday Parties by Kooky

the leash until her new-found desire for discipline diminishes.

Dear AFGHAN LANDERS,

My "little sister" (that's what my family calls her, but I can assure you, that Silky Terrier hell-on-four-paws is no relation to me!) is driving me insane. Between her tearing through the house yapping at the top of her lungs, and chewing on Master's best oriental rugs, and peeing on the hard-wood floors, I'm a nervous wreck. I'm too old for this. How much trouble could I get into if I, say, bit off an ear or two?
—*Irritable Igor*

Dear Igor,

How much trouble? Too much! Take my advice and get a hold of your human's Xanax instead.

JUST SAY NO!

Dear AFGHAN LANDERS,

I am a little Lhash and I love to chew up Beanie Babies. My addiction has landed me in the doghouse more times than I can count. It's not the Beanie flavor, smell or texture I crave—it's their soft, furry vulnerability. When I feel a fresh B.B. struggling between my jaws I feel like a Doberman—so buff! My mistress says this is a bad habit, the children have tried to pull out my teeth, and Master has threatened to ban me from the house if I don't stop it. What should I do?
—*Beanie Addict*

Dear Addict,

Your need to dominate small, defenseless, bean-filled animals in order to feel buff indicates deep-seated emotional issues of control that probably began on the milk line, and that you are still struggling with now. I strongly urge you to seek professional help with your problem before you end up a toothless garage-dog.

Dear AFGHAN LANDERS,

My problem is that I'm a bit of a collector, always have been. It runs in the family—we are all Retrievers of one sort or another. Compared to the rest of my family, I'm pretty selective—I only collect bowling balls, rubber gloves, boxing gloves, glass milk bottles, Baby-On-Board signs, and used BBQ grills. Still, I'm afraid Master finds this avocation of mine unacceptable. Can you recommend a good 12-step program for me?
—*Packer*

Dear Packer,

Some humans (and it sounds like yours is one) need to open up to the joys of collecting. They need to purge themselves of their sterile, ascetic ways and learn to indulge life and its commensurate chaos. Rather than putting yourself through the 12-step mambo, I'd like to see you try some behavior modification techniques on your master. Keep on bringing that gold home; someday he'll see its value!

I'M AN EXCELLENT DRIVER

Dear AFGHAN LANDERS,

How can I convince my master to let me drive the car? I know I could do it—I'm a very cleaver Sealyham Terrier! Every chance I get I climb onto his lap and put my paws firmly on the steering wheel. But he just chuckles and puts me back on the passenger seat. How do I prove to him that I really am an excellent driver?
—*Car Crazy*

Dear Crazy,

Have you considered how you plan to push the pedals?

Dear AFGHAN LANDERS,

I'm half Great Dane, half Saint Bernard, and I am hopelessly in love with Boris, the handsome Pomeranian across the street. Be honest, is there any hope for us?
—*Extra-large But Lovable*

Dear Loveable,

In situations such as yours, where there is true love there is always hope, and usually a ladder. The most unlikely couple I ever knew was a female Newfoundland and her Maltese mate; they've had four healthy litters so far.

Dear AFGHAN LANDERS,

If dogs have to wear dog licenses, why don't people have to wear people licenses? Isn't this species discrimination? Should I write my Congressdog? Who is my Congressdog?
—*A Political Pet*

Dear Pet,

It's a good question. There is no good answer. Let it go.

BETWEEN THE SHEETS

Dear AFGHAN LANDERS,

Sometimes my master and mistress hide under the covers and wrestle and growl at each other. I've tried to break up their fights, but they either ignore me or yell at me to be quiet. I don't want to end up the victim of a broken home. I think they need professional counseling. What is your opinion?
—*Worrying & Wondering*

Dear Worrying,

Your master and mistress are not fighting, they are simply looking for lost contact lenses.

Dear AFGHAN LANDERS,

I am a middle-aged Airedale and I like to bark and point my nose at people who fart. Is there really anything wrong with me?
—*Nosey Parker*

Dear Nosey,

By Dog standards, no. By human standards, you are a perverted, disgusting, and embarrassing Dog to have around. Learn to control your fart fetish if you want to stay in your family's good graces.

Dear AFGHAN LANDERS,

I'm a Labrador suffering from a severe case of Lab-lunge, which is, according to *Webster's*:

> LAB-LUNGE (lŭnj) n. The uncontrollable tendency of Labrador Retrievers to make sudden forward movements in response to anything they believe to be edible.

My master says I would eat myself to death, given half a chance. What I want to know is, how can I get half a chance?
—*Big Boy*

Dear Big Boy,
Dream on!

NATURAL REMEDIES *for* WHAT AILS YOU

COMMON SCENTS AROMATHERAPY

by Aromahund

Pungent garbage
cures constipation

Ripe laundry
soothes separation anxiety

Stinky cowboy boot
alleviates athlete's paw

Find out more about how
Common Scents Aromatherapy
can help you live a more scentual life.

Call 1-800-SMELLS
right away for a free, scented brochure.

Oh Boy!
Oh Boy!

It's the DOGS' LIFE
SCRATCH 'N SNIFF page

Paw here... and sniff Can you identify the scent?

Can you identify the scent?

Send your answer (only one, please) to:

DOGS' LIFE magazine
Scratch 'n Sniff Contest

the **Mate** market

DOGS SEEKING BITCHES

The Big Easy!—Handsome, athletic Black Lab, 4 years young, 110 totally buff lbs., is seeking playful, foxy, 1-2 year old white Toy Poodle for running on the beach, chasing squirrels, and tipping over garbage cans with. *Dagwood*

Can You Teach This Old Dog a New Trick?—I am a mature Cocker Spaniel who enjoys crotch sniffing, short walks and random barking sprees. I am hard of hearing but easy to please. Interested in meeting any old bitch. *Duke*

Toy With Me—Super-charged Aussie pupster needs hyperactive playmate for fun and games and the usual mayhem. Must love herding. *Zippy*

Hard Working—Professional St. Bernard widowed with pups. Hobbies include woodcarving. In need of a tender-loving bitch for long-term relationship. *Bernie*

Beagle Boy!—I don't bite, whine, bark or scratch, but if you're the right bitch for me I will beg. Must be long-legged, friendly and faithful. No fleas, please. *Norm*

ACME PATERNITY TESTING

Are you a single bitch who:

✤ Is unsure of who the father is?

✤ Wants to be certain about her pups' pedigree?

✤ Is tired of whining at that deadbeat doggie dad who claims not to have fathered all those hungry mouths sucking at your teats?

✤ **CALL 1-800-WHODAD**

Me Hung Low—Chinese Shar-pei. New in town. I have not flea. Am sexy guy. For good times, you call me. *Lik Sin*

Lassie Come Home!—I am an extremely unattractive but honest and intelligent little house Pug. Interests include toilet paper, table legs and meeting a beautiful, sophisticated Collie bitch of puppy rearing age. *Maxwell*

Hush Puppy—Laid back Basset Hound with lovely tenor voice is in need of sweet young thing to make beautiful music with. *Wagner*

Wild & Woolly—Slovenly Old English Sheepdog in need of affectionate bitch with comb. *Hairy*

Puppy Love—Playful, outgoing, lovable Scotty pup is looking for a bold & brazen bitch to teach me the facts of life. *Sugar Ray*

Placid But Romantic—Coonhound in mid-life crisis, in need of a sweet young bitch. Breed, color, size and bad habits unimportant. *Bubba*

Certified Mental Case—Energetic yet easy going, ambitious but apathetic, hardworking but lazy. Slightly schizoid Weimeraner. Interested in stable, meaningful short-term fling. *Jake*

Top Dog—Mature All-Male Mastiff. Intact and ready to party. *Boomer*

Dances With Wolves—And I don't mean fox trot. Single, professional, purebred Dalmatian, non-chewer, house-broken; looking for single pedigreed German Shepherd for mature relationship. *Gomez*

Full Of Love—Spiritual Tibetan Terrier with good chi, seeks female of the species for companionship only. *Dali*

Amoré—I am French Poodle recently retired from zee professional escort service, seeking charming female toy of any breed. *François*

Wild One—Howl at the moon? Sleep under the stars? Eat raw meat? Me: *Tarzan* the Pekingese. You?

A Real Winner—Clumber Spaniel. Runner-up at '87 Westminster Show, would really like to sire a litter before I kick off. Must be un-spayed. *Potter*

A Dog Named Sue—Creative and Crazy Akita (into cross-dressing) seeks any large bitch with excellent wardrobe. *Constantine*

Bright Eyed and Bushy Tailed—Neurotic Springer Spaniel enjoys obsessing about everything. I have warm paws and will remember you long after you leave me. *Louis*

Life in the Old Dog Yet!—Well endowed, "mature" Siberian Husky seeks slim, young female for a quickie behind the barn. *Alpo*

Intact and Unattached—Extremely good-looking Rottweiler with excellent fangs seeking mate who enjoys Tupperware parties. *Franz*

Not the Brightest Bulb in the Box—but big and lovable. *Bigboy*

Pound Hound—Long-haired mutt with blue eyes and a full tail. I am house-broken, non-chewing, non-digging, down-to-earth. Interested in mixing it up. *Tchumsa*

Let's Set Tongues Wagging!—Me: extremely studly, purebred Brittany Spaniel with impeccable pedigree. I hunt, herd, retrieve and play cricket extraordinarily well. I adore classical music by a roaring fire, exploring English garden mazes, and agility trials. You: purebred English toy bitch, 1 to 2 years old with similar interests. *Ringo*

Roam-Antically Inclined—If you are a sly and foxy female who likes to roam the back alleys in search of garbage, we should meet. *Guy*

Think Continental—Self-secure French Bulldog enjoys nude sun-bathing, drinking from the bidet, and growling at English dogs. *Napoleon*

Let's Get Down and Dirty—If you like mud baths, dig dirt, and relish rolling in anything rotten, I'm your Dog! *Bear*

Professional Pet Therapist—Whippet seeking unstable, psychotic bitch with lots of bad habits to test Freudian theories on. *Tachy*

Prize-Winning Sight Hound—Looking for my ultimate lure! Could it be you? *Clayton* (P.S. I'm tall, dark and handsome, too.)

Chow—Name's *Hannibal*. Call me.

Pick of the Litter—SWM (Single, White Maltese). No mange, fleas, ticks or doggie breath. Seeking new friend to share my bed. *Prince*

Too Much to Ask?—I am a Purebred, Champion West Highland White Terrier. If you are a full-figured, registered bitch of puppy-bearing age, well-groomed, intelligent, cultured, and docile, I may be interested. *Pomeroy*

Cold Paws Warm Heart—Professional Iditarod sled team dog seeking beautiful bitch to bring me in from the cold. *Gulliver*

Lap Dog—Middle-aged Shih Tzu: loves yapping, napping, snapping, and lapping. *Yu-Wu*

BIG—Good-looking mastiff would love to slobber all over you. *Utah*

Entertain Me!—I'm a clever little Jack Russell who likes crossword puzzles, game shows, magic tricks, and day trading. Your breed and size are not important, but you must have a high IQ. *Elvis*

Imagine—Middle-aged, professional German shorthaired pointer with a fetish for polyester and wingtips, and a strong need to control people. Seeking compliant, obedient bitch to act out bizarre fantasies. *Klingbile*

Miniature (in name only)—Schnauzer with fascinating pedigree. I'm very well behaved and love to chase dust bunnies. *Cupido*

I Watch Gopher Burrows…all day, except to come in and eat. Lately though, I've been thinking of having sex. If you think you might be interested in a Basenji like me, please call. Thanks a lot. *Chester*

BITCHES SEEKING DOGS

Flea Bags Need Not Apply—Single Schipperke seeks serious relationship with sexy Silky Terrier. *Agatha*

Speak Up!—Youthful, energetic, excitable Pomeranian bitch would love to meet a yappy male to bark with all day long. *Gloria*

Be My Beast—Beautiful, naturally blond Chihuahua with a strong sex drive and no phobias seeks romantic encounter. *Madonna*

Want a Cookie?—Now that I have your attention: I am a hungry Hungarian Puli seeking an energetic, tall dog with good dumpstering skills. Call *Zsa Zsa*

Full-Figured Dachshund—Into Tootsie® Rolls and daytime soap operas. Looking for height-challenged dog to share sofa. *Biffy*

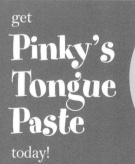

Help Me Please!!!—I am a high-strung, overly verbal, bug-eyed Pug in desperate need of a calm, understanding, patient male. *Yappette*

Want To Be Handled?—I'm the Queen of Control, the Dominatrix of Domestication, the Royal Bitch of Restraints. *Martha*

Long-legged & Sexy—Irish Setter is desperately seeking a four-legged stud muffin to roll over and lie for. *Bonnie*

Too Good To Be True!—Shy, playful, affectionate mixed-breed female wants to meet a loveable boy dog to share bones (and more?) NO DROOLERS, PLEASE. *Aphrodite*

Swim Away With Me—Petite Newfoundland would like to meet a Portuguese Water Dog to swim with me to Bermuda. *Esther*

Be My Pet—I am a hip and sensual 5-yr. old Bolognese, into yoga, jazz, and serious partying. *Evita*

Dominant—Female Brussels Griffon requires brainless, malleable male for M&M games. Will consider any purebred toy. *Suzette*

House Mate Wanted—Lonely Lhasa Apso looking for live-in lover. Bad habits a plus. *Lilly*

Gold Digger—Gorgeous, well-mannered Dandie Dinmont Terrier with excellent pedigree, desires to meet a well-heeled dog of considerable financial means. *Vanessa*

Happy as a Dog With 2 Tails—That's what this bitch will be when she meets her dream dog: a tall, dark and handsome brute with big balls and lots of other toys. *Cookie*

Looking For Love—The unconditional kind. Confused and slightly handicapped Afghan-Dachshund bitch seeks supportive, loving male lap dog. *Wilma*

Bow Wow WOW!—Crazy Dingo bitch, loves Frisbee, Nerf balls, hide 'n seek, and all other games. Need playmate NOW! Must be very fast and very furry. *Dixie*

Are You?…a handsome Silky terrier, 1-2 years old who is picky about his food and enjoys constant yapping? Meet your other half! *Octavia*

Roll Over!—I'm a cute, un-spayed, sex-starved, Papillon love puppy—very into panting and heavy petting. *Pandora*

DOGS SEEKING DOGS

Mischievous—Mutt loves to play games in well-equipped dungeon with rolled newspapers, choke collars, leather leashes, and more. Obedience training also available. Must be up to date on shots. *Ben Dover*

Fun-Loving Puli—Into pillows, lingerie and fly paper. *Ernie*

Gay Dog—With a serious fur fetish and lots of naughty toys. I'm in the market for a cute, new playmate with NO obsessive/compulsive chewing disorders. *Hoover*

Dog To Dog—Find out what it means to be with a Real Dog. Masculine, aggressive and passionate Corgi with excellent wardrobe is seeing Boy Toy for discreet relationship. *Rupert*

Get Shorty—Miniature Pinscher. 3 yrs. 6 lbs. Big ears. Likes spicy foods. *Rachmaninoff*

Son of a Bitch—Wild and crazy Cavalier King Charles Spaniel has cool pad and fabulous shoelace collection. Willing to share it all with the right dog. *Chuck*

Dog Friday—Discrete Pharaoh hound would like to be your slave and get you all hot under the collar. *Friday*

BITCHES SEEKING BITCHES

This Lady Lost Her Tramp—Now that he's finally out of my hair, I'd like to meet a stable, well-adjusted, thoughtful bitch to roam the mall with. *Floe*

Gorgeous, Sophisticated & Brilliant—Also, ambitious, bossy and loud Yorkie bitch interested in narcissistic female for mutually beneficial relationship. *Hillary*

Butch Bitch—Forming all-bitch Bull Dog club for organized dumpster raids. *Hilda*

Looking For One Fine Bitch—Must be stubborn, kinky and smelly. *Geraldine*

the classified Dog

ITEMS FOR SALE

Tennis ball collection—All major brands in mint condition in original cans.

Doghouse—Andrew Lloyd Wright-style as depicted in Barkitecture. Sacrifice price–I am not worthy.

Rare collectable—Scat the Cat Beanie Baby, slightly chewed and missing a few beans.

Medium choke collar—Will consider trade for sex.

Master's Slippers—Size 14-C, Macgregor plaid felt with soft faux fleece lining, in pretty good shape.

Imported Persian Rug—Thick, plush, exotically scented, with long fringe, and only minor "staining."

Tickets to upcoming SPCA Cat Show. Sacrifice price.

Tasty, well-used cookbooks splattered with bacon grease, cookie dough, enchilada sauce, and more. Will trade for used wooden spoons.

Super-Dog costume with cape, size XXS and never, ever worn by THIS Super Dog!

Tupperware—Succulent, pliable, stackable containers and lids. Clear and colored, incomplete sets, some unwashed. Bargain prices.

Brandy Keg with collar. No brandy left, but keg in chewable condition.

Barbie Doll—Mithing an arm and thome hair, but sthill highly dethierable.

Skateboard—Dangerous, but fun.

Electronic Husband. Cord slightly frayed. Please call after dark.

Moving Sale! Must sell entire collection of toys: Rhino-Bones, Chew-'n-Squeaks, Plushy-PlayPalls, Rope-Creatures, and Jolly-Balls. Toy chest included if you take the lot.

Water Pic—Marvelous fun for fangs and gums, especially when plugged in.

Rear fender off Classic '55 Chevy, slightly dented but very little rust.

Rare petrified Persian hairballs—Serious inquiry only, please.

Aged baby diapers—100% cotton (not the disposable kind.) Call for availability.

A+ Homework: Plato's complete works, complex mathematical proofs, comparative anatomy sketchbooks, chemistry lab notebooks, and more. Excl. condition. Masters Degrees also available.

BBQ Grill. Well seasoned and hardly licked.

Mommy's Brand New, all Leather, Yves St. Laurent satchel, in excellent condition: Must sell quick.

KY Jelly—Effects unknown. Will trade for Oinker Rolls or Freeze-dried Liver Treats.

Radial tire, some tread left. Delivery included.

SERVICES

Little Spot's Excellent Marking Service: 4 months' experience. Bonded and very reliable.

FAST Cat Chasers—available for immediate hire. Reasonable prices.

Are You Financially Secure? Do you know where your next bowl of kibble is coming from? Find out what your owner's financial status is. Order your copy of "Financial Report of Your Own Owner" today. Confidentiality guaranteed.

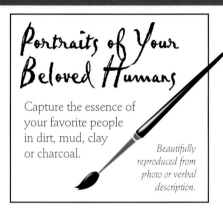

Big or Small—We Chew it All—Beaumanchew Masticators, Inc.

Fantasy Pedigree Papers—Our authentic-looking lineage certificates are handsomely printed on expensive-looking cream-colored parchment, suitable for framing. Please provide details of desired family ancestry. Send for yours today and be the dog you've always wanted to be.

HELP WANTED

Excellent Pay! Easy Work! Disassemble products at home.

Experienced diggers wanted for ambitious landfill project. Must be motivated!

Don't just sit there! Hundreds of businesses need Good Dogs, now! Immediate openings for service, entertainment and companion Dogs. Send resume to Jobs-For-Dogs Inc.

SnipPet Dog Grooming School has immediate openings for groom-able dogs: No experience necessary. Must be lazy, hedonistic and enjoy being fondled by excited humans.

the classified Dog

BUSINESS OPPORTUNITIES

Get Paid for Barking at Strange Noises: Start your own Watchdog Business. We'll show you how.

Flea Circus For Sale
Trained fleas included.

Millionaire Reveals: Amazing money-making secrets! Send $1,000 or 250 lbs. Milk-Bones.

RAT LOVERS!
Selling lucrative ratting & moussing business.

Great income.
Terrific exercise.

INSTRUCTION

Drool like a St. Bernard in just 3 weeks: Learn at home with our easy home study plan.

Be a Security Dog! Study in the privacy of your own doghouse and learn how to search pockets, purses, briefcases, diaper bags, etc., for dangerous and/or edible items.

Tired of always being on the short end of the leash?

Learn how to explore on your own the **Roamer's** way.

Send for your free catalogue of
Roamer's Travel Guides

LOST AND FOUND

FOUND: Cheap wig—long, red and frizzy. Well worn especially the bangs.

FOUND: Computer mouse with 18" tail.

LOST: Old beaver pelt and cowhide sporran (that thing Scotsmen wear around their waists). Great sentimental value. Last seen: Caramel Scottish Highland Games.

FOUND: On top of Mt. Om: Meditation mat of maroon velour w/gold tassels.

LOST: Lap–soft, warm, and very friendly. Missing for days, I'm desperate. Please HELP!

LOST: Herd of 53 prime Merino sheep in various sizes and colors. Last seen on side of hill. If found please corner but do not alarm. BIG REWARD!

FOUND: Extra-large boxer shorts in Donald Duck print with well-developed fraying and staining patterns.

LOST: Cute brown and white tail, about 8-inches long. Missing since last week's vet appointment. Can't wag without it.

no bull.

BodyGuard Services
vicious. tough. dependable. cheap.
CALL 1.800.nobull

Inflatable Laps

Comfortable, warm, convenient,
and *so affordable*

Call for a free brochure
1-800-BIGLAP

Dumb DOG

trivia game

Name these famous dogs:

Chance	1. The main dog character in Jack London's book, "The Call of the Wild"
Astro	2. The three-headed dog guarding the gates of Hades in Greek mythology
Martha	3. The dog in the movie, "The Grinch Who Stole Christmas"
Wolf	4. The American Bulldog in the movie, "Homeward Bound"
Toto	5. The Golden Retriever in the movie, "Homeward Bound"
Bullet	6. The Brussels Griffon in the movie, "As Good as it Gets"
Duke	7. The Jack Russell Terrier in the movie, "The Thin Man"
Tiger	8. Dorothy's little dog in the movie, "The Wizard of Oz"
Honey Three Evil Eye	9. The real name of "Eddie" in the TV show, "Frazier"
Cerberus	10. English poet Lord Byron's beloved Newfoundland
Moose	11. The Golden Retriever in the movie, "Air Bud"
Butkis	12. Family dog in "My Three Sons" TV show
Bingo	13. The first dog in space, aboard Sputnik 2
Lady	14. Odysseus' dog in Homer's "Odyssey"
Petey	15. The dog on every box of Cracker Jack
Krypto	16. The original Little Rascals' dog
Boatswain	17. The Brady Bunch's family dog
Bruno	18. Spuds MacKenzie's real name
Tramp	19. Walt Disney's family Poodle
Ruff	20. The Beverly Hillbillies' dog
Verdell	21. Paul McCartney's Sheepdog
Asta	22. The Simpson's family dog
Buck	23. Dennis the Menace's dog
Argus	24. General Patton's Bulldog
Willie	25. The Jetson's family dog
Buddy	26. Rip Van Winkle's dog
Max	27. Roy Rogers' dog
Santa's Little Helper	28. Cinderella's dog
Shadow	29. Superman's dog
Laika	30. Rocky's dog

check your answers on page 91

DUNCE

STYLE

the doggie cologne

answers

to Dumb Dog Trivia Game/Name the Dog

1. Buck	11. Buddy	21. Martha
2. Cerberus	12. Tramp	22. Santa's Little Helper
3. Max	13. Laika	23. Ruff
4. Chance	14. Argus	24. Willie
5. Shadow	15. Bingo	25. Astro
6. Verdell	16. Petey	26. Wolf
7. Asta	17. Tiger	27. Bullet
8. Toto	18. Honey Three Evil Eye	28. Bruno
9. Moose	19. Lady	29. Krypto
10. Boatswain	20. Duke	30. Butkis

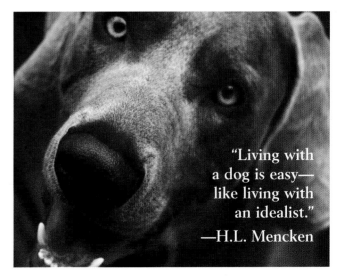

"Living with
a dog is easy—
like living with
an idealist."
—H.L. Mencken

January
3rd: Festival of Sleep Day
8th: Animal Care & Well-Fair: Savannah, GA
14th: Dress Up Your Pet Day

February
International Friendship Month and National Snack Food Month
17th: Random Acts of Kindness Day
25th: Quiet Day

March
1st Week: National Professional Pet Sitters Week
18th: Pets go to work in place of their owners
21st: National Tree Planting Day

April
National Garden Month and National Humor Month
1st: Share a Smile Day
28th: Arbor Day

May
1st Week: National Pet Week
Mid-May: Be Kind to Animals Week
18th: Visit Your Relatives Day

June
3rd: Pet Parade: La Grange, IL
3rd Week: Take Your Pet to Work Week
18th: International Picnic Day

July
11th: Cheer up the Lonely Day
18th: Cow Appreciation Day
21st: National Junk Food Day

August
3rd: Friendship Day
15th: National Relaxation Day
21st: National Homeless Animals Day

September
Mid-Sept: National Dog Week
13th: Positive Thinking Day
28th: Good Neighbor Day

October
Adopt a Shelter-Dog Month and National Cookie & Dessert Month
National Animal Safety & Protection Month
29th: Wild Foods Day: Pikeville, TN

November
8th: Cook Something Bold and Pungent Day
13th: World Kindness Day
2nd Week: Pursuit of Happiness Week

December
15th: Underdog Day
26th: National Whiners Day
27th: Visit the Zoo Day

dog days

mre DUMB DOG TRIVIA

1 What is the fastest breed of dog, and at what speed has it been clocked?

2 What did the docked tail of an Old English Sheepdog used to mean?

3 Where is the longest dog fence in the world and how long is it?

4 Where does the phrase "raining cats and dogs" come from?

5 Where does the term "Three Dog Night" come from?

6 How many dogs survived the sinking of the Titanic?

7 How many times is "dog" mentioned in the Bible?

8 How many dogs served in the Viet Nam war?

9 Where does the word "puppy" come from?

10 What breed was Lt. Colombo's dog?

11 Where did Rin Tin Tin come from?

12 Where is the Dog Collar Museum?

13 What is the Beagle Brigade?

14 What does BARF stand for?

a Rin Tin Tin wanna-be

answers to MORE dumb dog trivia

1. A Greyhound, which has been clocked at 41.7mph.

2. That it was a working dog and also exempt from taxes.

3. In Australia. It is almost 6,000 miles long (over 1,000 miles longer than the Great Wall of China), made of wire mesh and barbed wire, and is used to keep wild dingoes from killing sheep.

4. During torrential rains in 17th century England, many cats and dogs were drowned and floated down the streets, making it appear to be "raining cats and dogs."

5. From Australia, where the Aborigines slept with dogs year round. On especially cold nights they needed three dogs to keep warm.

6. Two dogs survived the Titanic; a Pomeranian and a Pekingese.

7. "Dog" is mentioned fourteen times in the Bible.

8. The confirmed count is 3,747, but as many as 4,900 dogs may have served in Viet Nam.

9. Most likely it comes from the French word *poupee*, meaning doll.

10. Columbo's dog was a Bassett hound

11. Rin Tin Tin was rescued from a German war trench by U.S. airmen at the end of WWI. He went on to make over 40 films and earned over $1,000 a week.

12. In Leeds Castle in England, with a collection of the finest dog collars from over five centuries.

13. The Brigade is a team of about 40 Beagles used by the U.S. Department of Agriculture to sniff out prohibited foods arriving in baggage from abroad.

14. It stands for Bones And Raw Foods, or Biologically Appropriate Raw Foods, thought by some to be a healthier diet for dogs.

acknowledgements & photo credits

Thanks to: all the wonderful dog owners who allowed me to photograph their dogs; Saxon Design for creativity, helpful suggestions, and patience; Melinda Mathias-Porter for careful editing and thoughtful phrasing; Laren Bright for some inspired wording; Massey's Camera, Williamsburg, VA for photographic assistance (and 1,000 MilkBones); "Ma" Ernie Eberheardt for all kinds of support; Bob Stein for use of his classic cars; and especially to Gary for love, laughs, and always believing.

Unless otherwise noted, all photos are by Heidi A. Ott. Key: Page #, Ad or Article: Dog's name (Owner's name).

Front cover, Woodie (Pam Simons).

Page 1, YAP: Gigi (Meg Lockwood); Buckwheat (Marilyn Sanders).

Page 3, Compulsion: Danny; owned and photographed by Lorie A. McCrone.

Page 4, Table of Contents: Jack Russell terrier is Buster (Jennifer Gibbs).

Page 5, Table of Contents: "Table Scraps" Pugs are Molly and Spunky (Kathy Routten); "Playtime" Aussies in truck are Corkie, Amber & Valerie (Karen & Russ Brickner).

Page 6, About Our Contributors: Rover Washington is Chilli (Jade Sikes); Smellany Post is Deena (Annie Grace); Mooch Fillmore is Chase (Jody & Tony Fecondo); SheBear de la Laisse is SheBear (Elise McConnell); Dr. Baily MacGrowell is Baily (Cindi Arain).

Page 7, Just chew it!: Pebbles (Jennifer Brown).

Page 8, A Letter from the Alpha Editor: Boo (Heidi & Gary Ott).

Page 9, Club Shed: Riley (Marie and Greg Goble).

Page 10, Dear Dogs' Life: Snow Dog is Cody (Eric Ryziw), Frisbee Dog is DalKai (Doniel Schwartz).

Page 12, Deli Raided: West Highland white terrier photo by Carol Thompson; Jack Russell terrier is Holly (Jennifer Gibbs); Norfolk terrier is Jade (Mary Jo Sweany); A Little Lower Please: Dillon (Cassie Brill).

Page 13, Chung's Depilatory Cream: Chung (Candy M. Stephens).

Page 14, Buster's Balls: Buster (Jennifer Gibbs).

Page 15, Tails of Woe: Chow is Emelye (Kim Bowden).

Page 16, Well-Bred Shredding Company: Toby (Pam Davis).

Page 19, Toilet Paper for Dummies: Wolfhound is Stella (Janet Queiser); Pugs are Molly and Spunky (Kathy Routten); Shis Tzu is Gizmo (Karen & Russ Brickner); Lab is Mousse (Aleta Channell).

Page 20, Soap Opera Reviews: "As the Tail Wags," Henry and Morgan (Kay Routten); "Days of Our Dogs," Bridget (Jill Vaden).

Page 21, Dogue: Emmitt (Shanen Costanzo).

Page 22, Taste Test Results: Wally (Mary Anna & John Bryant); Snowflake (Toni & Mark Treworgy).

Page 23, Dogs' Life Sports Page: Sebastian (Ellen Parkin); Cosmo (Melody Daniels).

Page 24, The 7 Habits of Highly Effective Beggars: Daisy (Katie Rust).

Page 25, The 7 Habits: Trixie (DeWaun Countryman); Blixen (Kelly Holland); Bridget (Jill Vaden).

Page 26, The 7 Habits: No Bull (Michelle Morris); Striker (Marie Stewart); Que (Cheryl Munker).

Page 28, Chicken Soup for the Bowl: Kourtney (Anita Pearson).

Page 31, Dogs' Life Readers' Survey: Boss (Aleta Channell).

Page 32-33, Dog Park Etiquette: all photos taken at Quiet Waters Park, Annapolis, MD.

Page 34, Shar-Pei Wrinkle Creme: Daisy Mae Flower (Elizabeth A. Proffitt).

Page 35, Are you a Good Dog…or a Bad Dog?: Zoey (Jo Bisbach and Steven Kipphorn).

Page 37, Fire Hydrants of France: Treavor (Michelle Massie).

Page 38, Bark-A-Lounger: Buck & Elle Mae (Carolee & Jason Spradley).

Page 39, Dog House of the Month: Annie (Theo Togstad).

Page 41, Off The Beaten Path: Brady the Shelty (Trudy McLain); Zip the Border collie (Peggy Stein); Ben the Lab (Jim Harrison); and Bob Stein, the chauffeur.

Page 42, Muttivational Posters: "Attitude," Shameus (Holly & Bill Wolfe); "Persistence," Rachael (Jill Vaden).

Page 43, Ask an Australian Shepherd: Daemon (Averill Ring).

Page 44, Pookie's Diary: Dayna (Jessica Ortiz).

Page 45, Party on the Bone Phone: Justice (Cheryl Munker).

Page 46, Boxers: Jewels (Mary Jane Dinges).

Page 47, Leash-less In Seattle: Ozzie (Shirley Meyers).

Page 56, Lab Coats: Boo (Heidi & Gary Ott); Miller Lite (Jennifer & John Lawson); Chelsea (Sterrie & Fran Weaver).

Page 58, Canine Academy: Que (Cheryl Munker).

Page 65, Master's Card: Jager (Mark Bunn); Help Yourself Books: Bravo and Brandy (Shannon Bowman).

Page 66, Why Table Legs Turn Us On: Jenna (Mary Lee Duncan).

Page 67, Table Legs: D'Bo (Heather Trantham).

Page 68, Reggie's Excavation Service: Annie (Theo Togstad).

Page 71, Pembroke's School of Herding: Will (Vonda Winkler); AARF: Annabelle (Kay Routten).

Page 72, Peaky Wants to Know: Peaky's photo by Carol Thompson; Saint Bernard, Ballerina Whippets and Tootsie Roll dog photos by Jan Lachenmaier; Cowboy Border collie is Bravo (Shannon Bowman).

Page 73, Arthur Furray's Studio of Dance: Treavor (Michelle Massie); Hand-Held Chewing Supplies: Holly (Sheryl Clifton).

Page 74, Wanted by the FBI: Hector (Kathy Nowak).

Page 76, DogGone Answering Service: Prophet (Cherie Smith); Lucky's Bail Bond Service: Trell (Dick & Marie Johnson); Crotch-Sniffers Anonymous: Oakley (Marilyn Sanders).

Page 77-78, Your Canine Sign: Aries the Airedale: Blitz (Stewart Pennell); Gemini the German Shepherd: Dolly (Delia Sapiro); Cancer the Collie: photo by Carol Thompson; Virgo the Vizsla: Zoey (Jo Bisbach and Steven Kipphorn); Libra the Labrador: Hershey (Sam Dempsey); Scorpio the Scottie: Sallie (Donna L. King); Sagittarius the Soft-coated wheaten terrier: Shameus (Holly & Bill Wolfe); Capricorn the Cocker spaniel: Jason (Jill Vaden); Pisces the Poodle: Diesel (Ann Hayward and Bill Walker).

Page 79, Play Date of the Month: Molly (Kathy Routten).

Page 80, Afghan Landers: Lizzietwist (Sylvia Broderick).

Page 81, All Dressed-Up: photo by Jan Lachenmaier; Birthday Parties by Kookie: Hector (Kathy Nowak).

Page 82, Just Say No: Pebbles (Jennifer Brown).

Page 83, Common Scents Aromatherapy: Eskimo Dog is Tantor (Ellen Parkin); Bloodhound is Dillon (Cassie Brill); Pugs are Molly & Spunky (Kathy Routten).

Page 84, Scratch 'N Sniff: Maggie (Donna Mercer).

Page 85, Acme Paternity Testing: Pug is Gigi (Meg Lockwood); puppy is Reba (Ann Summerford).

Page 86, The Mate Market: Sonja (Teresa and Noel Pyle); Boo (Gary & Heidi Ott); Pinky's Tongue Paste: Lexus (Kim Bowden).

Page 87, Dogs with stick: photo by Keith Pelletier.

Page 89, No Bull BodyGuard: No Bull (Michelle Morris).

Page 90, Dumb Dog Trivia Game: photo by Jan Lachenmaier.

Page 92, Dog Days: Pug is Princess (Meg Lockwood); Corgies are Will and Tucker (Vonda Winkler).

Page 93, More Dumb Dog Trivia: Pug is Molly (Kathy Routten); Bloodhound is Dillon (Cassie Brill); "Rin Tin Tin" is Jager (Mark Bunn).

Page 95, Dedication Page: Photos by Jan Lachenmaier.

Page 96, Publisher's Weakness: Boo (Gary & Heidi Ott).

Back Cover, Got Milk-Bones?: Cody (Marie Stuart).

Elise McConnell.
This book is dedicated to her.

For Elise, life was never about becoming rich or famous—although in her own way, she was both. Rather it was about the joy of living intensely every day. Being utterly independent, wonderfully creative, amazingly artistic and dangerously mischievous, Elise created innumerable adventures, both for herself and for her family and friends. Those experiences were always extraordinary, sometimes dangerous, and invariably hilarious. Like the time the Chinese hamster she smuggled home from China (in her pants) became agitated and bit her in the crotch as she stood in line to pass through U.S. Customs at LAX. Or the time she "kidnapped" a friend for a surprise birthday celebration and, while speeding down the freeway, was pulled over by two F.B.I. agents concerned about why the car's passenger (Elise's "victim") was wearing a pillowcase over her head. Or the time she dressed up to play "Brown Beard the Pirate" for her nephew's birthday party, and nearly lost her right hand to a short-fused firecracker.

For Elise, everything was cause for celebration: the solstice, a birthday, a homecoming, landing a job—even losing a job—April Fool's day, the full moon, a new puppy.

SheBear, her little black Schipperke, was rarely far from Elise's side. They hiked the foothills of their home town, Santa Barbara, California, took long bike rides (the dog in a backpack), and, occasionally, Elise even took SheBear out on training paddles on her out-rigger canoe.

Elise traveled the world—but not via the usual routes. She loved a challenge and knew no boundaries. She had a million friends, and was a best friend to many. Her spirit lives on in her many works of art, in the boxes of costumes she created to fool and amuse her friends, and, especially, in the fond memories of all of us who loved her.

"Life is a creative process."
Elise McConnell (1955 – 1998)

"Dogs are the most amazing creatures; they give unconditional love. For me they are the role model for being alive."
—Gilda Radner

Publisher's Weakness!

hint: dog treats

Boo Ott, publisher of **DOGS' LIFE** magazine, invites you to send in your own cute, clever and amusing stories and photos, along with a dog treat, for possible inclusion in the next issue of **DOGS' LIFE**.

Guidelines:

1. Attach your story and photos to a yummy dog treat and send to:
   DOGS' LIFE magazine
   Department DOG TREATS FOR BOO
   311 Jethro Lane
   Yorktown, VA 23692
2. Include the following contact information: name, address and phone number, and email if you have it, of you and your human.
3. Put your story on a CD or a floppy disk; please do not send the story via email. And definitely do not send dog treats via email.

Tips on taking good doggy pictures:

1. Use 35mm slide film (best), or print film (okay), or, if you have to use a digital camera, set it at the highest resolution and largest size possible. Then send an electronic file on CD or floppy disk plus a print.
2. Wash your face! Eye boogers are not attractive to our readership.
3. Try to get the horizon level, not all askew.
4. The background should be clean and simple, without a lot of big human feet, ugly furniture, and other unnecessary stuff to distract from the main subject—you, the dog. Dog treats, however, look good in pictures.
5. Make sure you do not have a telephone pole, tree, or similar object "growing" out of the top of your head.
6. Take a bunch of photos and send in the best ones.
7. Try to be in focus.
8. Don't forget the dog treat.

Hints for sending dog treats:

Milk-Bones, Pupperoni, Beggin' Strips and PIGS' EARS are Boo's favorites!

Please note:
All dog treats become the property of Boo Ott, and all photos become the property of his company, Riverbank Press. The Cat will scan your photos and slides. If Boo really likes the dog treat you send, your entry stands a good chance to be used in the next issue of DOGS' LIFE. If your entry is used, you will get a free, autographed copy of the magazine (but you will not get your dog treat back).

Woof, and good luck!

Boo Ott